Also Met

Along the Way

MORE SHORT STORIES ABOUT PEOPLE IN VERMONT

❧

Cornelius "Con" Hogan

D0067817

2008

MANUFACTURED IN THE UNITED STATES OF AMERICA

Library of Congress Control Number 2008935397
ISBN 978-0-915010-49-3

For ordering information
or to purchase additional copies, please contact
EAST HILL FARM
324 GONYEAU ROAD
PLAINFIELD, VT 05667-9669
chogan@conhogan.com

Designed and published by
SUTTER HOUSE
P.O. BOX 212
LITITZ, PA 17543

To

ASHLYN AND OLIVIA

Contents

About the Author -- 7

Preface --- 9

Up and Down Action -- 11

Do You Know What You Are Doing? -------------------------------- 12

The Best Builder's Insurance That Money Couldn't Buy ----- 15

The Breaking Point -- 17

Hoisted by His Own Petard -- 19

Pat Leahy and the Skinny-dippers ----------------------------- 21

Ed Sawyer and the Radar Base----------------------------------- 23

The Houdini of Vermont-- 27

Reporters Are Human Too-- 30

I'm In Charge Here --- 32

Governor Salmon and the Dark Desk --------------------------- 35

The Red Stamp -- 38

Night Porter—More Common Sense Than Most People --- 41

John Buik and the East Corinth Trail Ride -------------------- 45

Governors Are Real People Too --------------------------------- 49

Mickey Gallagher, Charlie Lewis, and Capital Punishment-- 52

During the Week I Work for Richard Snelling --------------- 55

I Have the Power to Pardon-------------------------------------- 57

A Man of Few Words --- 62

A Man Who Would Not Accept 'No' ----------------------------- 64

Deane Davis—It's the Little Things ---------------------------- 66

Strange Things Happen When It Gets Cold in Vermont ---- 68

It's Miller Time--- 70

'Perfect'-- 72

Here's What I Think of the Lottery Bill--------------------- 74

Neil and the .22-- 75

Asparagus --- 77

Governor Snelling's Late Musings------------------------------ 79

A Remarkable Memory--- 82
Lady Jeannette--- 84
Joe, It Was So Good To See You------------------------------- 86
The Jackaphesalope-- 89
Ultimate Justice -- 93
Finding the Common Ground----------------------------------- 97
Bob Murray ... Over Time-------------------------------------100
Afterword ---103

About the Author

Cornelius "Con" Hogan and his young family moved to Vermont in early 1972 from central New Jersey where he had spent seven years of work in corrections, beginning as a Correction Officer. He spent another seven years in that work in Vermont as Deputy Commissioner and later as Commissioner of Corrections.

He and his wife, Jeannette, and daughter, Ruth, along with Kathie and Bill Moulton, their farm partners, operate East Hill Farm Family Riding Center, which was established in 1976 in Plainfield, Vermont. The Hogans' son, Neil, and his family also live on East Hill Farm.

Over the years they became part of a remarkable neighborhood of self-sufficient people, many of whom had roots going back to a much earlier Vermont.

In his professional work, Hogan was fortunate to have worked in five different administrations of four different governors of both parties, ending his government career as Secretary of Human Services under Governors Richard Snelling and Howard Dean.

Today, he is an international consultant on children's well-being issues, working in far-flung places such as the U.K., the Netherlands, Australia, Chile, Ireland, Norway, and, most recently, Northern Ireland.

Throughout his life in Vermont, Con and his family have enjoyed and savored the independence and character of everyday Vermonters and their leaders.

Con is also the author of *At the Crossroads: The Future of Health Care in Vermont* and *Met Along the Way: Short Stories About People in Vermont*. He is hoping that this book, *Also Met Along the Way: More Short Stories About People in Vermont*, will be a worthy successor to the earlier book.

Preface

The success of *Met Along the Way: Short Stories About People in Vermont* was truly a surprise. More than 2,000 Vermonters purchased the little book over the months after its publication in September 2005. As I traveled throughout the State, meeting people at bookstores and other gatherings, I heard several common themes in many of the comments that people made about the book.

First, I was quite surprised about how many of the people written about were known to other Vermonters far and wide. Vermont is truly a neighborhood in the scale of things. Secondly, the book unleashed a torrent of stories from people who have their own stories to tell, but who have never taken the time to write them down. Finally, many told me that these stories represented a bit of a respite from our fast and complex times. The stories caused some to stop and reflect on the more memorable characters who had made an impact on their lives. These reactions and responses were gratifying to say the least. They also caused me to take the next step of sharing more stories.

As I reviewed a late draft of this, the second effort, it became clear that some of these new stories had broadened into longer essays that were beyond simple moments and events. This second round sometimes expands into trying to capture the essence of one person or another based on a broader view of events and time. I also included two descriptive excerpts from pieces I had written many years ago that today have additional meaning but had little apparent purpose at the time.

I believe the many readers of *Met Along the Way* perused the book with considerable enjoyment. But I have to admit … I'm having fun too.

Acknowledgments

This second little book came together a little bit easier than the first effort, which "got us on a roll," but it still required the help of several others.

Doug Livingston, owner of Sutter House, who designed and applied his publishing skills to the project, is still trying to teach the author the basic do's and don'ts of publishing. He is getting close to succeeding.

Tim Newcomb, who also provided the caricatures for the earlier *Met Along the Way*, continues his high level of creativity with this book. His good humor and skill are greatly appreciated by the author.

My wife, Jeannette, once again tempered my exaggeration factor by bringing many of the stories back to reality. Together we had great fun in remembering these vignettes.

And a final thanks to all those who took the time to send me notes and letters with ideas for this second edition.

Up and Down Action

A story about Bill Cowles, the first Secretary of Human Services, was the lead story in *Met Along the Way*. As a result, Bill contacted me. He's now in his 90s and living in Santa Fe, New Mexico. Since the first book was published, Mr. Cowles and I have had a terrific correspondence. The following is a tidbit about Governor Deane C. Davis from a conversation that Bill had with his boss, the Governor.

In 1970, Governor Davis, who was quite the horseman, was talking about a particularly annoying legislator who had been giving the Governor a hard time in the press on an environmental issue. Davis' comment to Bill Cowles was that "this man is like a horse I once owned and later sold ... that had plenty of up and down motion, but made little forward progress."

Do You Know What You Are Doing?

In the first edition of *Met Along the Way*, there were several stories about the very wise and experienced Governor Deane Davis. The Governor's known wisdom and common sense has been captured in several books, including *Justice in the Mountains*, published in 1980 when the Governor was 80 years old. It was the Governor's chronicle of his early and extensive time as a public servant, primarily in his work as State's Attorney. His offices at that time were in Barre, Vermont.

As mentioned in the first book, the failing Windsor Prison was one of his banes.

I hadn't been in Vermont in my new job as Deputy Commissioner of Corrections for more than a month when there was a serious blow-up at the prison. There were no hostages in this particular event, but any time fundamental control is lost by the keepers and taken by the inmates, the basic instability of the situation can rapidly turn dangerous. My boss, the Commissioner of Corrections, unfortunately was out of Vermont at that time, so it fell to me and the Deputy Secretary of the Agency of Human Services, the now well-known Bill Gilbert, to whom I would report in a situation like this, to head directly to the prison to take stock and support Warden Bob Smith in any way we could to bring things back into control.

Part of Bill Gilbert's job was to communicate directly with the Governor to keep him apprised as to what was going on, while I spent my time with the warden figuring out the next steps to regain control of the prison and make sure that no one got hurt in the process.

About an hour after we arrived at the prison, Bill came into the captain's office, which was located just off what was known as "B Block," one of the three housing blocks for the inmates. He told me that Governor Davis, who was at his home in Montpelier, wanted to speak with me. I followed Bill back out of the security section of the prison and into the administrative section, which housed the warden's office and was where the Governor was waiting on the line for me. What followed was one of the more extraordinary conversations I have ever had with any public official at any time in my long career of government service.

Governor Davis: "Bill tells me that your name is Cornelius Hogan. Is that correct?"

Me: "Yes, sir."

Governor Davis: "Cornelius, have I met you yet?"

Me: "No, sir."

Governor Davis: "What is your position in the Department of Corrections?"

Me: "I am the Deputy Commissioner of Corrections, sir."

Governor Davis: "Cornelius, how long have you been in Vermont?"

Me: "Thirty-two days, sir."

At this point the Governor paused for quite a while as he was obviously thinking through about who he was dealing with at this rather tense and important moment.

Governor Davis: "Cornelius, how long have you been in your job as Deputy Commissioner?"

Me: "Thirty-two days, sir."

Now, there was an even longer pause.

Governor Davis: "Cornelius, how old are you?"

Me: "Thirty-one years, sir."

At this point, there was an extraordinarily long pause on the other end.

Governor Davis: "Cornelius, do you know what you are doing?"

Me: "Yes, sir."

At this point, it became clear to me that the Governor had made his mind up about me, because with almost no pause, he said, "Cornelius, I'm going to bed now. But I do want you to have Bill Gilbert call me first thing in the morning to let me know how all this turned out."

I had just experienced a taste of the well-known wisdom that was an everyday aspect of Governor Deane Davis' way of doing business.

I have worked in five different administrations in Vermont, and they were all extraordinary governors. But I'm willing to wager, and I have firsthand experience that leads me to conclude that every one of them would have had a state police escort bring them to the scene of the problem with the press corps close in tow. And, further, that they would immerse themselves into the moment-to-moment decision-making to direct and help resolve the problem. Deane Davis had full confidence in the abilities of the people who worked for him to bring things to resolution, and he did not carry a deeper need to be visibly part of the solution.

I hope that the legend of his overall wisdom has just been enhanced another notch.

The Best Builder's Insurance That Money Couldn't Buy

In the mid 1970s, Jeannette and I had decided to build our own home with the help of faithful friends—Gene Foss, Lynn Copeland, Topper McFaun, and the ex-farmer Joe Griffith, who lived just across Gonyeau Road and from whom we had purchased the acreage. At that time both of Joe's parents were still alive. Annie Griffith was well in her 80s and was considered the matriarch of the neighborhood. Nothing went on at East Hill of South Plainfield that Annie did not know about.

(Actually, since we were in Plainfield, East Hill was somewhat mis-named, as the real East Hill was on the northerly side of Plainfield, while the East Hill where we had our farm was called East Hill by people in Barre Town, since most of the hill was in Barre Town. But to add to the confusion, it should have been called South Hill, as the hill enjoyed an almost perfectly southern orientation that captured the maximum sunlight and made it a desirable place to settle.)

We proceeded by contracting out the digging of the cellar hole, having the cellar floor and walls poured, and the septic system installed. We were on our way.

It eventually came time to order the materials from Allen Lumber in Barre. Soon after placing the order, a large flatbed truck delivered the entire load of lumber and dropped the material at the site. A day or two later, an acquaintance at work suggested that I should have builder's insurance that would protect me from serious loss if, by chance, some night the materials disappeared.

It was something I had not thought about, and we didn't have many financial reserves at the time since we had put most of our savings into the building materials themselves.

We had already been doing family business with Paige and Campbell in Barre for other insurances. We specifically had become the client of Robert Batchelder, who had grown up on East Hill and is a hunter on the hill to this day.

I called Bob at his office and shared with him my concern about the safety of the building materials. Bob immediately chuckled and then asked me, "Con, aren't you building right across the road from the Griffith homestead?" "Yes," I replied. Bob then told me that he had grown up on the hill and knew the Griffith family well. He also knew of Annie's reputation of knowing everything that happened in the neighborhood. Basically, he told me that I did not need to buy builder's insurance because Annie and her binoculars would keep a close eye on proceedings at the new home site.

I was certainly relieved to know that my materials would be safe and that I did not have to spend the money on the insurance. Over the years I often thought of the irony of an insurance broker advising me not to buy insurance in that situation. And it also made me understand better my new neighbors, and the sense of safety and caring that they would spend on me and our family over the years.

The Breaking Point

In the first *Met Along the Way*, I introduced the readers to one Harold Muzzy, the longtime road commissioner of Berlin, who was our neighbor in the early 1970s when we lived on Muzzy Road. Muzzy Road was obviously so named because it was the site of Harold's and his wife, Pepper's, homestead, and the homestead of some of their relations.

At one point during that time, Jan and I decided to raise a few beef cows on the scrub acreage that was prevalent in the little valley. Harold helped us find three Hereford yearling heifers that we were able to purchase at a decent price. This was in early summer. The cows got along well, did well on the grass, and quickly gained heft and weight. By October, though, the three girls had decided that the grass indeed looked greener on the other side of the fence, as they had pretty well cropped down the grass on their side. One afternoon, we found them on the wrong side of the fence. A bucket of grain and an hour later, we had enticed them back into their pasture. But now they had had a taste of the untouched green grass on the other side of the fence, and they began to leave for the greener grass regularly.

We searched the perimeter of the old barbed wire fence, but we could not find the spot where they had been getting out. The cows didn't seem to have any marks or cuts on them, so it was clear that they had found a way to avoid the cuts and slices of the old barbed wire fence.

We were returning them now to their side of the pasture fence several times a day. The cows were beginning to be a greater nuisance, as they were now getting into Jeannette's garden that she had worked so hard to cultivate over the summer months.

One Saturday morning, Jeannette and our daughter, Ruth, who was in fifth grade at the time, were working in the terrific garden that had been such an attraction to the cows. Once again, the cows were spotted up the road on the wrong side of the fence. By now the cows had been conditioned to resist the temptation of the grain bucket, and it was taking longer and longer to catch them and put them back in the rightful place. It took a lot of time to walk them down the road and convince them that they belonged on their own side of the fence.

A half hour after the above escape, Ruth was looking up the road and saw the three cows, one after the other, actually jump over the barbed wired fence from the pasture onto the old dirt road. This time it took two hours to recapture the increasingly recalcitrant escapees.

Not a half an hour later, Ruth and Jeannette were on their knees in the well-tilled dirt of the garden, cutting Brussels sprouts and chucking them into bushel baskets. They heard a crunching sound behind them. When they turned around, here were the three cows with their noses in the bushel baskets, eating the Brussels sprouts as quickly as Jan and Ruth were tossing them into the baskets.

The breaking point had been reached. This time, instead of convincing the cows to proceed to the pasture side of the fence, they were loaded into a horse trailer and were on their way to Eric Velander's, the local slaughterhouse and butcher at Berlin Corners.

No beef we ever had tasted better.

Hoisted by His Own Petard
(a Gene Foss story)

Gene Foss was the long-standing budget director of the Vermont Department of Corrections. Prior to that, he was business manager at the Brandon Training School for some years. Brandon was a facility that was distinguished for serving the formidable needs of the severely disabled. In those roles, Gene knew the people of government in a way that few ever had during his time of service which spanned from the 1950s to the 1990s.

Gene tells the story of one particular director of purchasing for the State who was known for his penny-pinching practices. His approach was to buy the lowest price commodity and worry about the quality later. For example, this particular civil servant felt that the toilet paper being purchased by the State was too rich and that he could save the State money if he purchased in quantity a lower-grade paper.

After this new paper was distributed throughout the government center of Montpelier in all of the most important places in the State buildings and the State Hospital in Waterbury, it wasn't long before the purchasing director began to receive a steady stream of complaints from State workers, who on the whole, not being very well paid, tended to jealously guard their little prerogatives.

It turns out that the compulsion that the purchasing director had about price had deeper significance because,

19

during his term, the poor man suffered a bit of a nervous breakdown and found himself suddenly as a client of the State Hospital. His stay at the facility was only for a few days in order to stabilize his hopefully temporary condition. However, he did get a chance to experience firsthand, the results of his controversial purchase.

Gene recalls vividly that the first purchase the old purchasing director made after returning to his position upon his release from the State Hospital was to order enough higher-quality toilet paper to replace the low-cost paper that he had previously purchased.

State workers all rejoiced ... and all was well once again within the bureaucracy.

Pat Leahy and the Skinny-dippers

Patrick Leahy, Vermont's long-term and highly esteemed United States Senator, began his public service career as District Attorney for Chittenden County. According to Bill Cowles, Vermont's first Secretary of Human Services in the late 1960s, Patrick called Bill for some advice about a complaint that Leahy's office had received. The complaint was that some young people were skinny-dipping in a tributary of the Winooski River. (Winooski, by the way, is native Indian language for "smelly onion.") Leahy asked Mr. Cowles, in his role as Secretary of Human Services, to review the situation and report back to him on the subject.

After doing due diligence, and letting an appropriate amount of time pass, Cowles wrote a brief report to Leahy and solemnly determined that

the skinny-dipping was not a crime as it did not violate any Vermont law, nor was it a public health threat, nor was it even a public nuisance.

State's Attorney Leahy readily agreed, and the issue was put to bed.

This was a little victory for common sense in government. Justice and the social condition of Vermonters had been temporarily joined.

This little incident was a precursor to the common sense and gentle sense of humor that Senator Leahy has shown in his 30-plus years of service as a United States Senator in his service to Vermont.

Ed Sawyer and the Radar Base

Author's Note: This story was written in November 1978, after a visit to the East Haven Radar Base with George Wilson of WCAX-TV, who took marvelous photographs. It was submitted to Vermont Life *and its fine editor, Brian Vachon, for publication but was rejected because of a concern that the base was an "attractive nuisance," which held dangers for unauthorized visitors. Following is that article in full. The readers need to project themselves back to 1978 in order for the article to make the fullest sense. At this writing, the old radar base is once again in Vermont news, as it is the proposed site for a wind farm.*

On the top of a 3,400-foot mountain in East Haven, Vermont, in the heart of the Northeast Kingdom, stands a lofty, lonely sentinel, keeping watch over Unknown Pond, Victory Bog, and Paul's Stream. It is an abandoned radar tracking base built in the early 1950s by the United States Air Force. Much of the fascination with this base is rooted in its history and its current owner. However, its primary characteristic is a strange attraction born of its unnatural, almost eerie placement in one of the most unspoiled wilderness areas in Vermont.

The North Concord Radar Base, also known as the 911th Radar Squadron, was constructed at the height of the Cold War era. The stated purpose of the facility was "to provide search and height finding radar data under all specified modes of operation to the defense sector, and to eliminate or reduce the effects of deliberate jamming or interference during an emergency countermeasure environment."

The capital cost of the base was more than 15 million dollars. Soon after the base's completion, it was considered obsolete due to new satellite tracking technology and was abandoned in 1955. Even after the several hundred men left the base following its formal deactivation, nonbreakable, longer-term contracts for continued modification and continuous maintenance resulted in many more public dollars "invested" in an obsolete appendage of the military's space age communications network.

How does a citizen of the town of East Burke come to own an entire radar base complex? It begins with Ed Sawyer's dream of a splendidly isolated retreat in the peaks of the Northeast Kingdom of Vermont, then inquiries to the military, and finally the submission of a low bid of $42,500 for a facility described by the Air Force "as is" at a public auction in Boston, in the presence of only two half-serious bidders. Suddenly, in 1965, Ed Sawyer was the proud owner, c.o.d., of one brand-new radar tracking facility of the highest sophistication and technology known to man, located somewhere in the wilderness of northeastern Vermont.

Ed Sawyer is an active man who makes high-quality wooden toys for a living in his small shop on the main road in East Burke. His fertile mind projects rapid imagery, particularly when he is talking about his mountain, and what might have been. His possibilities for the mountain-top range from a massive revolving restaurant attracting people from as far away as Montreal and Boston to a place where corporation executives would participate in free-wheeling, free-thinking seminars in an unfettered environment.

East Mountain is about ten miles from East Burke. The climb to the top of the mountain is over a remarkably well-preserved military road. The road crosses the commencement of the Moose River and miles of land owned by the St. Regis Paper Company. At one point a beaver pond has washed out part of the road, and Sawyer's power wagon is carefully guided over a makeshift log bridge. Several hundred yards later lay the main base area, the cantonment, where the support systems for the summit operations were located.

During the first and second years after he purchased the base, Ed, his wife, Irene, and two-year-old son, Shawn, lived and worked in a woodworking shop in one of the 150-foot Quonset huts that previously housed more than 50 men. One can only imagine the lonely isolation of several hundred non-Vermonters in this harsh, stark environment. (To reflect this feeling, there is a 30-foot mural on one of the Quonset walls, depicting Chicago's Lake Shore Drive.) He describes the sounds of snowmobiles driving over the completely snow-covered hut, oblivious to the fact that the structure even existed, let alone that three people were living there.

24

Sawyer describes a series of vignettes about life on the mountain. He tells of his sheep that were raised in the gymnasium and steers roaming loose on the mountain that learned how to menace intruders. Even today there are some twenty pigs roaming free and approaching visitors for handouts. His description of a motorcycle club's ride-in to the mountain top brings back memories of the "easy-riders" of the early 1970s. It is almost as though the setting itself creates an expectation that the strange is accepted as natural and commonplace.

The local townspeople have had changing feelings about the area. The short-lived boom times when up to 300 personnel lived on and around the base offered only a fleeting glimpse of prosperity. The development of the mountaintop, followed by an unfulfilled and short half-life of the base left many in the area disappointed. The dreaming of Ed Sawyer did not compensate.

The site has also served as a magnet to a variety of vandals over the years, with the result being an accelerated deterioration of the appearance of the base.

It is several hundred more yards from the main base to the summit where the radar structures are located. The towers reach upwards almost 90 feet. The climb to the top brings the reward of a summer panorama.

The three-hundred-and-sixty-degree view begins looking southeast over the mist-filled valleys. Victory Bog, Burke, Lafayette, Washington, and Groveton are clearly seen as the view sweeps counterclockwise to an easterly orientation. Then comes Maidstone Lake and Unknown Pond (where the St. Regis deep green forests are only now being logged for the second time in Vermont's history). Toward the northeast, overlooking the Connecticut River Valley lays North Stratford, Monadnock Mountain, Gore Mountain, Lewis Pond, and a wilderness known locally as the Madison. Lake Seymore, Morgan, Lowell, Eden, and the rocky face of Mt. Pisca overlooking Lake Willoughby show to the north. The only evidence of civilization is in the west. Varied shades of green-quilted farmland surround the hamlets of Barton, Sheffield, and Sutton.

In contrast stands the steel and concrete structures. The technology of the support systems required for survival is formidable. Ice removal from the structures was accomplished with four fifteen-thousand-gallon tanks filled once every two weeks with number two fuel oil and powered by five two-hundred-horsepower diesel heating systems. Two radar buildings are located at opposite ends of the summit compound so their anti-functions of transmitting and receiving don't interfere with each other. Three ray-dome towers are the central focus of the summit operations center, their substantial box-beam bases drilled into sixteen feet of mountain bedrock. An artesian well, septic system, and operations center complete the array of summit structures.

Combined effects of the constantly changing temperatures, continuous condensation, wind, ice, and snow have taken their toll over the last fourteen years, but, overall, the facility has withstood these ravages in remarkably aloof and undamaged fashion. The facility, its engineering, materials, and overall technology represented the best money could buy.

It is truly a different world that seems to both attract and repel. The magnetic quality of opposites becomes clearer in the cavernous underbelly of the largest radar tower; for here, in a womb of technology are neatly arrayed one- and two-horse sleighs. The spare and warm early New England lines sharply contrast to the stark mid-1950s military architecture.

The summit is an eerie place. The constantly moving air interplays among the forest and the abandoned structure. One is easily affected by the detached and lonely feeling of melancholia. It is an unnatural mating of steel and forest in a primeval setting.

There are clear signs now that the mountain is reclaiming its own—signs that underscore the fading of Mr. Sawyer's dreams. He hopes that somehow this mountain miscreant can be yet a place of enjoyment for many. We are left with a sense of great waste. This sense is sharpened as we view the base above from the lower exit road. This space-age dinosaur stands in bas-relief against the greenness of this beautiful mountain.

Exploring Vermont for its contrasts can be extremely rewarding.

The Houdini of Vermont

Windsor Prison was on its last legs by the spring of 1973 when it received a Canadian inmate, late of the notorious Laval Prison in Quebec. Wayne Carlson had a long history of criminality, much of which was enhanced and prolonged by one remarkable skill, namely his ability to repeatedly escape from seemingly secure settings and situations.

All of his escapes were bold, with perhaps the most memorable being his escape from the Chittenden County courthouse when he used a fake wooden gun to commandeer a sheriff's deputy and his real gun. He then took another deputy hostage, stole a car, and, after a high speed chase on I-89, ditched his hostages and disappeared for a few days in Burlington before he was recaptured based on an informant's tip.

After his third escape in Vermont, Carlson's fame was now statewide and beyond. There emerged a Wayne Carlson fan club and Wayne Carlson T-shirts with "The Houdini of Vermont" on the back. Vermont newspapers covered him with almost a kind of Robin Hood fascination approach. There were people actually rooting for him to get away as he made one escape after the other.

And these escapes in Vermont did not include others from his time in prison in Canada. He was a successful evader, not only of Vermont law enforcement but also of the Royal Canadian Mounted Police and the FBI.

His last two escapes were from Windsor Prison, which was billed as Vermont's only maximum security prison. On the occasion of his second escape from Windsor, on a Sunday afternoon, he waited for shift change. There were twice as many staff on duty during the time when one shift of custodians came on duty while the existing shift was going off duty. Later investigation reports from the prison detailed how his wiry frame was able to negotiate a supposedly unscalable wall of the prison, climb onto the slippery slate roof, and then clamber down the front of the building using a drain pipe, finally reaching a car that had been left for him and which he used to quickly disappear into the Vermont countryside.

My wife and I happened to be in Montreal that evening, on a short holiday, when we turned on the television. There was one of Montreal's prominent newscasters intoning something to the effect that "Wayne Carlson, late of the Laval Prison, has successfully made his fifth escape from Vermont authorities. It is widely feared that he on his way back to Quebec." His fame was now international.

One of my favorite recollections of the Carlson saga was after his recapture following the fifth escape. Arrangements were made with the Canadian government to return him to Canada, with an exchange to occur at the border. Patrick Leahy was the prosecutor in Chittenden County at the time and, like all law enforcement in Vermont, could not wait to see Carlson go. He wanted to make sure that the transaction with the Canadians was safely completed. I remember a call from Patrick on a Saturday morning, informing me that he would personally be accompanying the heavily armed and ample phalanx of State Police, Windsor corrections officers, and Chittenden County law enforcement personnel so that he

could see with his own eyes that Carlson was truly back on Canadian soil and gone from Vermont, where Carlson had made such an embarrassing shambles of law enforcement.

Fred Stetson was a reporter for the *Burlington Free Press* who covered the five brazen and creative Carlson escapes over the course of just eight months. In the 2003 February issue of the *Vermont Sunday Magazine* of the Sunday *Rutland Herald* and the *Times Argus*, he updated Vermonters on the life of Wayne Carlson. Thirty years after Carlson's remarkable escapades he has become a prize-winning author about prisons, including an autobiography entitled *Breakfast with the Devil*. He is now a family man who even has been in almost affectionate contact with some of the law enforcement people in Vermont from whom he escaped and led on chases throughout the State's byways.

That's the thing about human nature. Even though we like to believe we know what the future holds for certain people, one can never be sure. That is certainly the case with the life of Wayne Carlson, "The Houdini of Vermont."

Reporters Are Human Too...

In the 1960s, Mavis Doyle was a reporter with the Vermont Press Bureau. Bureaucrats lived in fear of Mavis, because she had a penchant for exposing their mistakes ... and their pay. She published the salaries of every appointed non–civil service servant and pointedly made sure that the reader knew the percent increase in salary from year to year, particularly if it was in excess of the increase that ordinary civil servants received. She had a tough-as-nails reputation and had cultivated contacts in government who would always give her the tips that she needed to expose the wrong-headedness or just plain egomania occasionally displayed by political appointees in government. Almost all of the people I came in contact with in Vermont's government had felt the wrath of Mavis at one point or another in their careers.

In fact, she was a legend in the press world and government. Her investigative work over the years was so solid that the Mavis Doyle Award is now given annually by the Vermont Press Association to Vermont reporters and journalists who have made exceptional contributions to the world of investigative reporting.

Somehow or another, over the years I had escaped her wrath. My name never showed up on the front page of the *Barre-Montpelier Times Argus* under Mavis' byline, and my salary was never prominently published along with the others. For a long time I kept my good fortune to myself, figuring that there was no need to stir a hornet's nest. Then one year, in the mid 1970s or early 1980s, after she had retired from journalism and I was out of government, I ran into Mavis on State Street in Montpelier. We had a very nice chat about things past, so during our talk I decided to take a bit of a chance.

I asked her why my name had not appeared with the other political appointees in the salary lists that she had regularly published. Her eyes lit up and she proceeded to tell me that her father's name was also Cornelius, and that whenever she saw my name as part of my work in government that it made her think of her father, and, well, that no one would notice that there was one less name on the published list than there should have been.

Mavis, like many reporters who carry a public persona of hardness and unapproachability, in that one moment, showed an interesting sense of softness beneath her hard exterior.

It was one of those delightful moments that you don't forget.

I'm In Charge Here

Other stories in the first volumn of *Met Along the Way* chronicled the tough times that Windsor Prison experienced in the early 1970s. During the administration of Governor Thomas Salmon, Windsor experienced yet another serious disturbance in 1973. On this trip down I accompanied Commissioner of Corrections Kent Stoneman. After we arrived at the prison, it was clear to see that things were well out of control. The inmates had taken over virtually all of the buildings inside the old granite block perimeter. This included the mess hall and the vocational building, where there was already a fire, along with some inmates rolling an oil barrel out of the automotive shop to be fuel for another fire that had been started in the yard. It was truly chaos.

At this time, Governor Salmon was out of the State of Vermont, and procedure in those days prior to our worldwide instantaneous communications capacity called for the Lieutenant Governor of Vermont, Mr. John S. Burgess of Brattleboro, to serve as the Acting Governor in Governor Salmon's absence. Burgess had an interesting political background, which included his having been Speaker of the Vermont House of Representatives.

It wasn't long before Acting Governor Burgess arrived at the old prison with an escort of state troopers.

My first recollection of Mr. Burgess' arrival was of him quickly climbing the stairs from the street entrance into what was known as the Control Area, which overlooked the entire inside perimeter of the prison. As the Acting Governor reached the top of the stairs, he was saying loudly to anyone within earshot, "I'm the Acting Governor ... I'm in charge here." And then, seconds later, he reached the Control Area platform, took one long look out into the yard and all of the chaos therein, then turned around and quietly asked, "Who's in charge here?" The Acting Governor had made a quick and accurate decision that he was in over his head, and he quickly got out of the way.

After a few minutes, Mr. Burgess approached me and asked if there was any way he could be helpful. I asked him if he had a camera. Governor Burgess indicated that he had one in his car. I asked him if he would take a set of pictures of any individuals whom he could see in the yard, and that the pictures would become important at a later date when inmates were being identified for prosecution. Acting Governor Burgess quickly agreed to do so, and I went on to other duties, not to see the Acting Governor again. He evidently left at some point during the day as the State Police slowly brought the prison back under control.

Several months later, I paid the Thrush Tavern one of my semi-regular visits after work, and there in a booth was Lieutenant Governor Burgess. He invited me to join him for a moment, and we had a quick chat. During our talk, I asked Mr. Burgess if any of the pictures he had taken had been developed. He said they had, but that they really weren't very useful. I asked why. Mr. Burgess told me that the camera he had in his car wasn't a very good one, that in fact it was an old "Brownie" box camera, which didn't have any telephoto capability. This meant that all of the human figures in the yard appeared as tiny little people in the photographs that had been taken at least 100 feet away. Further, Jack Burgess went on to describe that, because he had to take the pictures from inside the

control room, he had to take them through the vertical bars in the window. For example, he told me that he had taken a photo of an inmate who was climbing the flag pole in the middle of the yard in order to tie a pirate flag to the top of the pole, but, when the photo was taken, one of the black bars in the window was hiding the flag pole,

and the resulting photo was a picture of a tiny man climbing a prison window bar.

Jack Burgess was so very serious as he told me his story. He was so disappointed that he had let us all down with unusable photos.

I don't think there are too many other places in the country where such a high public official would have consented to take the pictures. And then tell the truth about how they came out.

Governor Salmon and the Dark Desk

Speaking of Governor Tom Salmon, the Governor, during his four years, had to face some very difficult fiscal situations, most of which were driven by the oil embargo of 1974. The embargo quickly plunged the State and the nation into a fiscal crisis, the size of which hadn't been seen since the Great Depression. But the administration made the best of it and made some courageous decisions about how to keep the budget in balance. One of the centerpieces of the Governor's strategy was to close the outmoded Windsor Prison and replace it with a set of smaller, less costly regional facilities. This resulted in the Commissioner of Corrections, R. Kent Stoneman, and his key people spending considerable time with the administration to assess the possibilities and to provide a never-ending stream of information to the administration to mollify the considerable number of critics of this bold move.

It was at the end of December 1973. As part of the information flow requirements, as Deputy Commissioner I was scheduled to meet with Governor Salmon in Montpelier at 9 A.M. on a Monday morning. However, I had taken a quick weekend to go visit my mother, who was very ill, in New Jersey. I took the old Montrealer, which in those days was a night train. That allowed me to travel Friday night to Trenton, New Jersey, and then catch the Sunday night train back, which would put me in Montpelier at about 7 A.M. This would give me plenty of time to get home, clean up, and meet with the Governor in his office on the fifth floor of the Pavilion Office Building, just next to the Capitol on State Street.

But the best laid plans occasionally have a way of unraveling.

I boarded the Montrealer as scheduled in Trenton, to begin the long ride north. What I hadn't taken into account was that this was the weekend that all of the students who had gone home for the Christmas holidays were now on their way back to college. Since the train would pass through White River Junction, it had been picking up students on their way back to Dartmouth College, which is a short distance from White River. I couldn't find a seat in the coach section, so I proceeded to the bar car, where, although it also was crowded, I found an empty seat. I made myself at home.

After we passed through New York City, the train was completely full, with not a seat available, and it was standing room only. It wasn't long before one of the talented students on board opened up the bar car piano, and soon it was party time. The party grew in numbers and intensity, and, of course, being in my early 30s at the time, I joined right in.

Hours of partying passed until about 3 A.M., when two things happened. First, the party had drunk the bar car dry, and the students were just beginning the process of drying out. Secondly, just outside of White River, the train came to a halt for some unknown mechanical reason. The stoppage resulted in the heat going off in the bar car and throughout the train. About an hour passed, and the bar car was getting colder by the minute. The outdoor temperature that early morning was 15° below zero.

You have never seen such a sad sack looking group of students who were slowly sobering up in a rapidly cooling rail car. The car also reeked of beer and sweat from the partying just a few hours earlier. We sat there for more than an hour. The thought began to sink in that I was going to miss my appointment with the Governor. Sometime after 5 A.M., the power came back on and the train began to move again.

The train finally rolled into Montpelier about 8:30 A.M., much too late for me to go home to Plainfield, clean up, put on fresh clothes, and get back to the Pavilion in time for the meeting. I had no choice. I had to go directly to the Governor's office regardless of my physical state and appearance.

I was dressed in khaki pants and a pullover shirt, on which both had been spilled some beer during the night of partying. I hadn't shaved for three days. I didn't look good, nor did I smell very good either.

My wife met me and drove me right to the Pavilion. I kept my ski jacket on as I headed to the fifth floor of the Pavilion. It was just 9 A.M., and I was escorted immediately to the Governor's office. In the middle of the rather dark office was a large, dark, oaken desk, which was brightly illuminated from above. It also illuminated the Governor, but the area

surrounding the desk was much less well lighted, and even darkened past the immediate perimeter of the desk itself.

I did my best to pull my chair somewhat back from the desk as we conducted the 15 minutes of prison business. My thought was that if I could remain more or less in the shadows, my appearance and beer scent would be muted. The meeting went well, and I got up to leave while the Governor remained seated behind the desk. As I began to move to the door, Governor Salmon, who was also known to occasionally party in those days, said, "Con, it was good to see you ... and I hope you had a good time last night."

There are some folks that one shouldn't even try to fool.

The Red Stamp

Tom Davis was the son of Governor Deane Davis ... but he was a Democrat and a long way from the Republican politics of his father. Today, Tom Davis is known as a fine writer of both fiction and nonfiction. Under his belt, he has a couple of excellent mystery novels that take place in the hills of Vermont and are presented in government settings. He is also distinguished for some of his writing about the Barre area and, in particular, old time baseball.

One of the most interesting appointments in State government was in the early years of the consolidated Agency of Human Services by Governor Tom Salmon. The agency had been created by Tom Davis' father, Governor Davis, just three years earlier. Tom was the second Secretary of Human Services, following William Cowles, who was featured in a short story in the first *Met Along the Way*.

Tom was Secretary when the very serious oil embargo hit the State's finances like a ton of bricks. Every Governor likes to indicate to whomever will listen that they were tight fisted with Vermont's finances and how careful they were with the taxpayers' money. But no governor in recent history was faced with the sudden and unpredicted shutdown of revenue from an economy that had stopped dead in the tracks of the embargo. For example, under direct order from the Governor, all agencies had to be on a 10% less spending track within 60 days of the order. Most government "cuts" these days are actually reductions from growth forecasts. These were real cuts to the current budget, and no one was immune.

In the Agency of Human Services, and in the Department of Corrections in particular, there were difficult choices to be made. The choice made by R. Kent Stoneman was to close the antiquated Windsor Prison, which had been declared unfit for human habitation by the Vermont Department of Health. It had been experiencing a string of spectacular escapes, including three by Wayne "Houdini" Carlson, a dangerous man from Laval, Quebec, whose story was recounted earlier in this little book. Kent's plans received solid support from Governor Salmon, Secretary of Administration Wilson, and Secretary Davis. There was a rapid coalition developing for this change consisting of both social reformers and fiscal conservatives, who made for strange bedfellows in this instance, but proved very important to the closing dynamics. (This dynamic has been captured by a classic little book, *The Closing of Windsor Prison*, by the accomplished oral historian Charles Morrissey.)

Secretary Davis worried about the ability of the machinery of State government to rapidly come to grips with the immense amount of personnel and construction paperwork that would be generated as a result of this bold move. So he came up with the idea to create a red rubber stamp, on which was emblazoned "Windsor Prison Closing." The stamp was to be used on every piece of paper that needed to flow into the bureaucracy to help make decisions and move the paperwork flow under the six-month project time line. It would include improving the local jails and regional facilities to handle the new load and reassigning about 300 employees to new work assignments, while at the same time protecting their civil service rights. There was also the work of reorganizing the management of the entire department in order to manage the new enterprise, in addition to filing reams of paperwork with the Law Enforcement Assistance Administration, which would be providing the operational bridge money above the already State-appropriated money for the prison. This funding would allow the operation of both the old and new systems for a short period of time and the implementation of new contracts with the Federal Bureau of Prisons, which had agreed to take some of Vermont's most dangerous inmates during the anticipated unstable transition. It was a massive and complex job that would involve thousands of documents, any one of which, if not attended to in a timely manner, could grind the project to a halt.

Governor Salmon's administration was populated with excellent people who were external to the Department of Corrections and who would be key to the success of the project. Some of the names that come to mind were: the Secretary of Administration, Bob Wilson; a key State personnel administrator, Sarah Philbrook; the Agency of Human Services Planning Director, Kathy Hoyt (who later would become Vermont's first female

Secretary of Administration under Governor Howard Dean); Richard Raymond, Director of Purchasing; Ron Crisman, State Budget Director, and many more who don't come to mind at this moment.

The paperwork flew through the bureaucratic thicket. Response times often came as a matter of hours instead of days. The red-stamped paperwork became a torrent through Vermont's government. And, remarkably, when the day was done, the entire project was completed on time and within budget.

I've often wondered if Tom Davis knew of the impact that his simple and straightforward idea had—creating a red stamp to help the normally balky State government hum like a well-oiled machine. In all the years that I served in and around government since then, I've never seen such a simple idea have such major impact; nor have I ever seen government work so well.

Maybe we need a little "red stamp" thinking these days.

Night Porter: More Common Sense Than Most People

Several stories in *Met Along the Way* dealt with people who ride horses, provide care for horses, or train horses. This is simply because horses have always played an important role in the lives of our family. We have owned and operated East Hill Farm Family Riding Center for more than 30 years now with our long-standing partners Kathie and Bill Moulton, and in recent years with our new partners, our daughter, Ruth Hogan Poulsen, and her Danish husband, Bo. There is no shortage of stories which can capture the highs and lows of being deeply involved with these magnificent animals.

This story is about Night Porter, a thoroughbred the farm acquired in the mid 1980s—a horse that became a very special part of our lives. Night Porter had been retired from the track after a modestly successful run and, in middle age, found himself in residence at Norwich University as part of the university cavalry program. He was generally an amiable horse of good size at about 16 plus hands, and he soon became one of the favorites of our daughter, Ruth, who rode him throughout Vermont in what is known as hunter/jumper competition. He was not without his faults. For example, for whatever reason, he would not allow anyone, no matter how much he trusted them, to pick up his hind legs. And it is important that a horse allow this in order to be properly shod, and, even more imperative, to allow proper foot care, which is essential to keeping a horse sound.

Even with this serious limitation, Night Porter remained healthy and, for some reason, always appeared to have well-proportioned and well-shaped hind feet.

When the farm was doing its own haying, we kept a rotary hay rake in back of the barn. The storage area for the rake was separated from the horses by two 2 × 4 rails.

One late winter's afternoon the snow had been sliding from the roof and accumulating at the base of the stall where the rake was stored. Porter was scrounging for bits of hay in that stall area. He evidently had his front legs on top of the packed and icy snow pile when he slipped, his front legs sliding into the rake stall and then into the rake itself.

This quickly became an increasingly serious situation. Porter was out of general earshot of the inside of the indoor arena where my wife, Jeannette, was teaching a lesson. Because Porter's body was straddling the snow pile, with his front legs now entangled by the rake, he could not muster the leverage to put his hind legs under him and then lift himself out of the increasing danger.

At that point, one of the young students came running into the arena to let Jeannette know that there was a serious problem out back of the barn.

We all took stock, and we knew that Night Porter was in serious trouble. Fortunately, I was in the barn, in the middle of evening chores, which consisted of watering and graining the horses. Also in the barn was our neighbor Lynn Copeland, who had been raised in the neighborhood and had gone to the one-room schoolhouse that now was on the lot next to our home. Lynn worked in the stone sheds as a heavy equipment operator, and we had developed a great friendship after we had moved to East Hill.

Lynn and I quickly came to the conclusion that if Night Porter was to escape relatively intact, that the hay rake, which was systematically tightening its grip on his legs, would have to be dismantled . . . in a hurry. But the only way to dismantle the rake was for the two us to slide on our backs underneath the machine and underneath Porter to remove the tines from the rake with wrenches. This was extremely dangerous because if Porter were to thrash and try to get out himself while we were underneath him and the tedder there was a very good chance we could become badly hurt in the process. To make matters worse, just before we began to slide ourselves under, Porter gave a mighty heave, and in the process swung his massive head, striking Jeannette and throwing her against the stall wall that she had been leaning on as she tried to quiet Porter by stroking his neck and talking in a soothing voice. It immediately became clear that she had broken some ribs.

Lynn and I slid under the tedder. We were inches from Porter's head above us. We could feel and hear the horse laboring and feel his warm

breath on our faces. We quickly worked with the wrenches. Porter didn't move a muscle during this time, although he was clearly in a position of pain. It was as if he knew we were in trouble too.

It is a well-known piece of knowledge about horses that if by chance they stumble with a rider on their back, or they don't make it over a fence while in a jumping competition with a rider, that they will do anything possible to physically avoid rolling on, kicking, or otherwise coming into contact with the rider on the ground. This is what Night Porter was doing at this moment.

Luckily, Lynn and I completed taking the two key bolts out of the hay rake at either end of the main bar that held the circular tines in place. At the same time, we were able to lower the bar down the other side of the snow bank, away from Porter. We quickly slid ourselves away, and immediately Porter found his front legs free from the imprisoning tines. With a mighty lunge backwards, Porter threw himself away from the tedder and out of danger.

But he was a mess. In the meantime, someone had called our faithful and long-term veterinarian, Dr. Tom Stuwe, who had arrived at the stable. Tom proceeded to put in place more than 150 stitches in the multiple cuts and deep scrapes that Porter had suffered while trying free himself.

Once again though, it was as if Porter knew the kind of trouble he had been in and was still in. He stood dead still, almost like a statue and Tom systematically put the stitches and staples in place so the healing process could begin.

It was a close call, but Porter had shown the common and quiet sense that horses can often show when under serious pressure.

Porter went on to have a wonderful career of show jumping over the next years with our daughter, Ruth. He was a special horse. He showed great poise under pressure—more poise than many of the people I've known would have shown if faced with similar circumstances.

John Buik and the East Corinth Trail Ride

Authors Note: The following is a shortened version of an article that first appeared in the Autumn 1977 issue of Vermont Life. *In effect, it was a tribute to John Buik of East Corinth, who by 2008 has run the ride for 37 years. Including this story helps bring home the point that we all need experiences such as this one to fully appreciate the place where we live.*

A slow drive through central Vermont on Saturday morning begins the weekend. The horses are nervously swaying in the van as we move across Orange Heights. An hour's drive brings us to East Corinth. Many of its 150 inhabitants live in the heart of town which sets on Tabor Branch just before it meets the Waits River.

The town consists of a single, white-spired church, a lone IGA store, working farms with residences facing onto the main street, related rural enterprises, a Masonic Lodge, a U.S. Post Office, one 7,000-unit chicken farm, and John Buik's Box B Ranch. The farm, reputed to be one of the most photographed in Vermont, is clustered around the main dwelling (circa 1797). This building is a collection of connected houses, sheds, barns, and other afterthoughts. John Buik, a breeder of roistered Quarter horses, is only the fourth owner since Colonel Goldsburn Taplin received the land in one of the original land grants giving by the King of England.

Pulling into the main driveway and through a natural arch between two of the farm buildings into an ample pasture behind the house, we are greeted with a gypsy-like atmosphere. Tents, large and small, are being pitched and camper units and pickup trucks are being set up to accommodate their owners.

By noon, the horses are being readied for the first day's ride. Riders of all sizes, ages, and riding styles and tacking a variety of breeds of horse, Palominos, Connamara ponies, Quarter horses, Arabs, Appaloosas, Morgans—all were represented.

The riders show a wide range of horse experience, from near novice to professional horsemen. They represent many backgrounds, including a contractor, farrier, deputy sheriff and police chief, small-business owners, government workers, teachers and college administrators, farmers, and many others.

By 1:00 P.M., almost 50 riders are mounted and await the trail leader. After a review of some rules of the ride that will make it a safe one, the ride begins.

The first day of the ride moves us upward onto Old Baldy Hill, behind East Corinth, to a panorama of the entire valley. Below us, to the west, lay the town, the Box B Ranch, and the green pastures in the center of an irregular frame of intense fall colors of the surrounding countryside.

After almost four hours and over 12 miles, the first day's ride is over and people and horses move stiffly as the horses are walked so they can cool properly.

By 6 P.M. there is the beginning of a chill in the air and small groups begin to wander down the road for the short walk to the Masonic Lodge where the Eastern Star of Corinth will serve a chicken pie supper. As the stairs are climbed to the second floor, we are greeted with a delightfully warm mixture of good food smells and friendly greetings. The hall naturally amplifies sound, and soon the accumulation of more than 60 high-spirited guests (some came just for the dinner) results in a happy roar.

Long rows of tables accommodate the diners, and with few preliminaries, the country-style meal is served. Heaping platters of steaming mashed potatoes, buttered peas, creamy cole slaw, and mounds of hot chicken pie are passed rapidly around the table. Waiters hover with pitchers of milk and coffee and quickly whisk away empty platters and, within seconds, reappear with more food.

A quick walk to the campsite under a nearly full moon and some tidying up around the camp site is followed by a check and some reassuring words to the horses. By now someone has started a large bonfire, around which campers begin to collect to counter the chill of the rapidly cooling night. Over the course of several hours many horse stories pass, along with some attempts at friendly horse trading. Some tentative barbershop harmony is heard in the background. The campfire holds most of the group together until the near-frost-level chill insistently prods some toward a last check of their horses and the warmth of their sleeping bags.

During the night, the crystal-clear atmosphere's effect on the warm land creates a dense ground fog, which settles gently into the valley and completely covers East Corinth.

It is early morning and the horses are restless, trying to stamp and paw away the chill accumulated during the night. They are also demanding to be fed. Those that are fed only feed the consternation of the others.

Suddenly, some marvelous coffee and cooking odors waft from in back of the house. The campers waste little time moving to where an outdoor cooking fire is in full blaze. Steaming coffee, orange juice, and homemade doughnuts hold off the first hunger pangs. Some of the group watch John Buik use an oversized camp frying pan to quick fry as many as a dozen eggs at a time. At the same time he is deftly turning strings of locally made Italian sausages.

By now, the sun is rapidly burning through the diminishing fog and casts the area in a shadowless intense white light. On a ridge behind the camp, a single tree, in full foliage glow, stands atop the fog, seemingly suspended without support.

Once again the horses are readied for about 15 more miles. The trailmaster leads the ride, single file, out of the pasture, across the road, behind the IGA store, and out to explore the westerly side of East Corinth.

Steadily moving upward, the riders reach one height after another, each offering new visual treats as we look southward over Corinth and West Topsham. Winding down from these high spots, the riders move through a steadily downward sloping stand of maples. The cheerful party crunches through the leaves as riders carefully avoid low-hanging limbs. Picking carefully through a pair of old wire fences, the riders move across a marsh area at the head of Blake's Pond. The pond mirrors the surrounding foliage perfectly. Maple leaves gently float, edges curled upward like the sails of tiny ships, and quietly move away from shore. The setting is so peaceful that many are reluctant to leave. Also, those who have been here before know that this point signals the beginning of the last stretch of the ride.

Coming out of the woods, the horses begin to sense that we are nearing home. They pull more steadily and the pace noticeably quickens.

It is only a matter of yards to the back of Page's Box Shop, which leans precariously over the Tabor Branch. We then move onto the main town road and in a few minutes are back at the Box B Ranch.

Now the ride's end procedures are less leisurely. Already, the thoughts of the riders extend beyond the ride.

The camper trailers and tents are packed for the trip home. The horses are subdued and resigned after two long working days. They load uneventfully, and after hurried goodbyes, we each go our separate way. But not before serious vows are made about making sure we will be back for next year's trail ride.

Governors Are Real People Too

Governors are real people in Vermont. … In Bill Gilbert's words, the best of them do not really understand the enormous investment that we ordinary mortals place in their every word and deed. And Bill provided the following story that makes the point.

As ordinary folks they fail to comprehend that because they won the election they have suddenly been recast by everyone except themselves into the persona of "THE Governor." From then on they might as well live on Mars, for they will always be seen and watched as we might watch an alien in our midst. Even a friendly, good-natured alien for whom we have campaigned has this remarkable aura once elected. Especially early in a first term, governors do not fully understand this aura or how it changes even a whisper of the governor into a shout or command.

Early in the first Snelling Administration, his new team was brought together at Seyon Ranch for a two-day planning retreat and team building for the new administration. Seyon Ranch is a lovely trout-filled pond owned by the State of Vermont, tucked in the hills of Orange County.

The appointed day arrived, and all enjoyed a spectacular, sunny day. Dinner and good informal discussions ended the day with great promise for a productive work session the following morning.

The next morning the Governor started us off with a lengthy review of his goals for the Vermont government during his first two-year tenure. He showed great facility on each of the subjects that he addressed. Governors are driven by the campaign process to know about virtually every subject that affects the lives of Vermonters. Richard Snelling, even more than most other governors, had rigorously prepared himself for the job. Everyone at the retreat understood that the Governor, in the words of Sister Elizabeth Candon, did "not suffer fools gladly." Most of the Governor's training came from his experience at Harvard Business School and his long years as a businessman, most recently as owner and CEO of Shelburne Industries.

Everyone was paying rapt attention to the boss.

To end his very thoughtful remarks, the Governor opened the discussion to the many commissioners and secretaries present. He asked that they join in and put their issues and plans out on the table for all to consider, and to develop and make the morning's work productive and an opportunity for all to strengthen their understanding of the many sectors of the responsibilities and policies of Vermont government.

Dick Saudek was one of Governor Snelling's new appointees. Dick is a very successful attorney who was then the very knowledgeable Commissioner and the Chair of the Public Service Board and Department of Public Service. He still is not and was not then a "shrinking violet." He was also a man who prepared himself well for eventualities like this one. He had prepared an outline of remarks regarding future energy policy for Vermont and was sure enough of himself to have volunteered to be the first Commissioner to present in front of the Governor. As expected, his presentation was logical, thorough, forward thinking, and was clear to all. He finished his remarks with a flourish and sat down.

All eyes then turned on THE Governor, who had listened intensely. After a considerable pause, the Governor said bluntly, "That proposal makes no sense at all, Dick." The silence was deafening. Lunch was almost three hours away but there were very few further volunteers to join the discussion after that.

In any other context with all of the same people in the room and Dick Snelling present as an ordinary peer, a great discussion of the issue would have followed this exchange. New facts would have emerged; policy would have been argued and improved. But Dick Snelling had just responded as THE Governor.

Governors often do not fully understand the power of their words and utterances. But Governors are human too.

Mickey Gallagher, Charlie Lewis, and Capital Punishment

In early 1977, I had just been appointed Commissioner of Corrections by Governor Richard Snelling. I was 36 years old, frankly a little young for this kind of assignment. However, I accepted the opportunity with relish. I had been the Deputy Commissioner under the marvelous Commissioner R. Kent Stoneman for seven years, and I felt ready for the responsibility.

It wasn't long before I received a phone call from WCAX to appear on the venerable Sunday morning half-hour news show "You Can Quote Me," a program that continues today moderated by Marcelis Parsons. The moderators at the time were well-known newscasters, the crusty Mickey Gallagher and the gentle and thoughtful veteran broadcast journalist Charles Lewis. The combination of the tart and sweet personalities always made the show interesting. Combined with the considerable homework and preparation that the hosts always exhibited, it made for a newsworthy half-hour.

Knowing that the hosts always had a thorough knowledge about the subject at hand created the need for those who were to appear as guests (like me) to do their homework well in order to be ready for the forthcoming inquisition.

To complicate my situation, I had never been on television before, and there was a growing sense of anxiety as my key staff worked hard to prepare me. This process can best be described as getting ready to answer "the ten questions from hell," with the underlying belief being that if those questions could be answered clearly and assertively then the odds of answering well any other questions that might be posed were high.

By the time of the Friday afternoon taping, which would be broadcast the following Sunday morning, I felt well prepared. And so the taping began.

Mr. Gallagher, in his typically gruff style, would typically lead with the question, giving the erudite Mr. Lewis the opportunity to pose the follow-up question while the interviewee was answering Mickey's leading question.

Things were actually going quite well. The prospect of filling an entire half-hour television show with solid and factual answers is at first quite daunting. But once the taping was under way, things seemed to move along quickly and well. At one point, I sneaked a glance at my watch and, to my surprise, the show was more than two-thirds over. I found myself thinking "this isn't so bad" when, out of the blue, Mr. Gallagher asked me what my position was about capital punishment. I simply froze. It was not a question that we had rehearsed or even thought about as we prepared. I sat in the hot seat silently and unmoving for what seemed like an eternity (although I'm sure it was only seconds) as the two pros waited for my answer, and in fact, any answer. Finally, I blurted out something to the effect that I did have a position on capital punishment but that "I'm not going to talk about it on the air."

Gallagher, to my great surprise seemed to have accepted that rather dumb answer and was moving on to the next question when the composed and urbane Mr. Lewis broke in with the following comment: "Commissioner Hogan, you hold a rather important policy position in the State of Vermont. Capital punishment is serious business, and you have the responsibility to share with our viewers your view on this important subject." This was as sharp an interrogatory as I had ever heard from the unassuming Lewis. By this time I had composed myself, and I quickly answered, "I do have a strong view about capital punishment and it is a closely held personal view. I am unalterably opposed to capital punishment for religious and moral reasons."

Both of these respected journalists accepted my answer, and we moved on to the next question and on to the end of the interview.

Monday morning at 7:30 A.M. I was in my office in Waterbury a little early, anticipating a call from Governor Snelling. The Governor had never made a big deal about capital punishment in his campaign, but he did leave it as an open question. And as a result of my answer I was expecting a call.

Our conversation began with the Governor complimenting me roundly on my overall performance in the interview. After that, though, he told me that there was one question that he would have answered a little differently.

Of course I knew what that question would be. He said, "Con, regarding the question about capital punishment, I would have said, if I were in your shoes, that as Commissioner of Corrections, that regardless of my personal views, I would follow the law … (and then he said with a sense of emphasis) *as long as I was the Commissioner."*

It was solid advice, with little room for not completely understanding the implications of what he was telling me.

Governor Richard Snelling was a mentor to many of the younger people in his administration. This was one of those "learning moments."

During the Week I Work for Richard Snelling

In *Met Along the Way,* I introduced the readers to Sister Elizabeth Candon, a woman who had an outstanding career as a teacher, Sister of Mercy, college president, and then as the Secretary of Vermont's Agency of Human Services. She was appointed by Governor Richard Snelling in his first round of service as Governor of the State in the mid-1970s.

It was clear early on, after her appointment, that her status as a Catholic Sister of Mercy would cause her some significant problems in her secular role as Secretary. The issue was straightforward and plain for all to see. The Catholic Church has an uncompromising position on abortion. In the eyes of the Church, abortion is the taking of a human life, and therefore a mortal sin. This issue has been at the center of and will continue to be one of the most divisive issues of our times. As Secretary of Human Services, Sister Elizabeth had ultimate responsibility for the State's Medicaid program, which allowed abortions as a medical procedure if agreed to by the client and her physician. This anomaly put Sister Elizabeth between a rock and a hard place—between her Catholic Bishop John Marshall, who headed the Vermont diocese, and her lawful duties associated with her role as Secretary.

The press, smelling the possibility of an ongoing controversy did their best to fan the flames. There were continuing articles in the *Burlington Free Press* about the issue, including a quite remarkable headline one day which blared to the effect that "Bishop Marshall Attacks Sister Elizabeth Candon."

Several reporters had tried to line up an interview on the subject with Sister Elizabeth, but for some months after her appointment she had simply avoided commenting on it. This made the press even more dedicated to getting the story.

At one point, there was a large conference in Burlington that resulted in Sister Elizabeth being one of the guest speakers. Elizabeth gave her talk, and then came the lunch break. Reporter Bill Felling of WCAX news was covering the event. He sent word to Sister Elizabeth that he would like to have a brief on-camera interview about the content of her speech. (The specifics of the speech elude me these many years later. This occurred early in 1977, almost 30 years ago.) Sister Elizabeth agreed, and soon she was in front of the camera and lights.

Felling jumped right in: "Sister Elizabeth, Vermonters want to know how you reconcile your being a Catholic nun and your being beholden to the canons of the Catholic Church, which as part of those canons, forbids abortion, which goes to your role in having direct responsibility for running the public abortion program through Medicaid."

There it was—

there was no avoiding the issue—in the bluntest language possible. Sister was trapped. … She had to answer.

After a short pause, Elizabeth smiled sweetly at reporter Felling and said the following:

"Bill, I'm afraid you just don't understand. During the nights and weekends I work for the Lord. During the weekdays I work for Richard Snelling."

She then smiled at the dumbfounded Bill Felling and quietly turned and walked away.

That was the last time the press tried to push the issue. Sister Elizabeth, through a combination of a quiet sense of beatitude, candor, thoughtfulness, and firmness, had won the day.

I continued to learn those kinds of lessons from her for many years.

I Have the Power to Pardon . . .

Every once in a while one has the pleasure and even privilege of seeing authority and power used in ways that make one admire the person applying it. In the winter of 1977 I had that privilege.

Richard Snelling ran for Governor on fundamental planks of fiscal responsibility and excellence in government. A lesser public plank was that during the campaign he made it known that he was not a fan of gubernatorial pardons, even though that power was vested in him in Vermont's constitution. Part of his overall view on the subject came as a reaction to the heavy use of pardons by the outgoing Governor, who was not running again, the highly regarded Governor Tom Salmon.

In addition to the fiscal skills that Governor Salmon showed as the nation's economy had suffered a brutal disruption during the 1974 oil embargo, which quickly affected State revenues, Governor Salmon carried a humanitarian streak for the underdog. And one of the underdog classes that the Governor took particular interest in were inmates, and particularly those at the Windsor State Prison, which at that time was the oldest continuing operating prison in the nation.

Governor Salmon made great use of a governor's power to pardon. He exercised that authority regularly, culminating in what became known as the Governor's Christmas Pardons. At its peak, pardons counted in the hundreds during the holiday season. The press had taken note of this practice, and Governor Salmon was under some public pressure regarding the practice. But given that this was the Governor's last term, he continued to pardon in unprecedented numbers.

Governor Snelling made it clear in the campaign that he did not like gubernatorial pardons. He considered them an irrational and non-objective way of making important decisions. He also felt that the pardon process had become somewhat abused, and that people should be released from jail by using the tried-and-true process which made the parole board ultimately responsible for the release decision.

When Dick Snelling appointed me as Commissioner of Corrections in early 1977, he said to me, "Con, I know you know my position on governor's pardons ... there won't be any." Since I had just been appointed by Governor Snelling to the position, and since I served at his pleasure, I readily indicated that I understood. One of my first acts as Commissioner was to let the corrections staff as a whole be aware of this new policy.

I soon learned that simply saying something is so does not automatically translate into practice. As time went on, I continued to receive requests for pardons from some staff, admittedly at a much lower number than had been customary in the past. In the corner of the old oaken warden's desk that had been sent to the central office of the Department of Corrections when Windsor Prison closed its doors in August of 1974, a small pile of these requests began to be evident.

I did my best to ignore this growing pile of cases for some months, but that just wasn't possible. In November 1977, I received a request from a contingent of respected probation and parole officers to meet with me in an effort to change my mind about the new policy. These people were the cream of the crop in corrections. They included highly experienced and effective people such as Steve Dale (currently the Commissioner of the Department of Children and Families for Vermont), Bill Young, Harold Stevens, Don Hess, Ray Thomas, and others who have faded into memory but who were known as high-quality and dedicated officers, and who had considerable morale suasion with the rest of the field force.

The ensuing discussion made it clear that in some cases, and some years ago, expectations had been set with some inmates and offenders that a governor's pardon was certainly possible if they kept their noses clean and took advantage of the educational and work opportunities available to them. Secondly, the probation officers made it clear that since the option of a governor's pardon was embedded in the State's constitution that I had a duty to advance these well-documented pardon requests to Governor Snelling for his consideration.

By this time there were 36 case files and requests for pardons on the corner of the desk. I took the views of these good people to heart and dedicated a weekend to reviewing each of these case files with a fine-tooth comb. I invited a few of the field staff who had paid me the visit to join me ... and several of them did.

We went over every case in detail and systematically boiled the 36 cases down to six cases, whose application for pardons were unassailable. I agreed to advance those six cases to the Governor. (After all, there had been more than 300 pardons approved by Governor Salmon in the previous year. Surely, I rationalized to myself, these six cases would be considered worthy by Governor Snelling ... although at the same time I had a sense of dread when I picked up the phone to call his office to ask for an appointment to discuss the applications.)

An appointment was made to meet with Governor Snelling. I had asked for a half-hour meeting, but the message came back that I would have all morning to discuss these cases with him.

I carried the case files, which were considerable, to the Governor's office in a carton, and at the appointed time I was invited into the Governor's office. His first words to me were, "Con, I thought we had agreed that there would be no pardons given during the time of my administration." I sheepishly agreed, but I then used the same arguments on the Governor, that the field staff had used with me. I broke through with the argument that since there was provision for a governor's pardons in the Vermont constitution, that I had a duty to bring worthy candidates forward, and that the Governor had a commensurate duty to consider them. The Governor reluctantly agreed to review the cases.

Before I had packaged the pardon requests, I had the common sense to put them in order from what I believed was the most difficult request to be the first one considered, down to what I had believed would be the easiest request to consider. So you can imagine how difficult the first request for the Governor.

The first case took the longest, but cases two, three, four, and five became progressively easier for the Governor to agree with and then sign off on. Then came the last case. This was an offender who was in jail for lewd and lascivious behavior. In other words, he had exposed himself in one of the shopping malls.

I suddenly found myself in an intense struggle with the Governor. We reviewed the case, and the Governor saw how hard this man had worked to obtain his undergraduate degree while in the custody of the

Commissioner. The offender had a perfect work record with glowing reports from his work supervisors. He had availed himself to a long-term treatment program to gain self-insight into his previous behavior. His family was willing to take him home and provide supervised housing. The pastor of his church spoke glowingly of the individual's newfound relationship with God.

The Governor was still reluctant to sign off. He asked me if I could "guarantee" that he would not re-offend. I said that no one could make that kind of guarantee, but that of the six cases we had just reviewed, that this case was far and above the better bet, based on the record, than the others we had reviewed and signed off on.

The Governor was impressed by the record on this case, and, as a result, he reluctantly agreed to pardon the man. In the middle of December, Governor Snelling signed the pardon papers and the young man was released from Windsor Prison as a free man.

Four days later, at 3:00 A.M., I was awakened at home by a telephone call from one of our probation and parole staff located in Morrisville. He informed me that the young man, who had just been pardoned, was picked up on the Stowe Road earlier in the evening, wearing women's underwear … and nothing else.

The sense of dread quickly returned.

When I reached the office at 7:30 A.M. that same morning, there was a message waiting for me that essentially said that the Governor wanted to see me in his office at 8:00 A.M. I made the drive quickly from our Waterbury office at the old State Hospital to the Pavilion in Montpelier, which housed the Governor's fifth floor office. I had also brought the young man's records with me.

Governor Snelling greeted me at the door of his office and told me to leave the young man's case file on the bench outside the door of the office, that I wouldn't need it.

I truly expected a serious dressing down from the Governor, who was somewhat known for being tough on his staff. And, given the inevitable working over the press was about to give the Governor for pardoning a "sex offender" when he had indicated that there would be no pardons in his administration and, further, having that offender re-offend within just a few days of the pardon was going to be politically painful to the

Governor—so it was not beyond my thoughts that I might even lose my job over this faux pas.

After I entered the office, the Governor approached me. When he was within a few feet, he looked directly into my eyes and said the following:

"Con, I simply wanted to tell you directly ... that as Governor of the State of Vermont, I have the constitutional power to pardon anyone I please. I used that authority in a deliberate and objective fashion. That is what I'm telling you ... and that is what I will tell the press this morning at my press conference ... and that is the end of this story."

That is what he told the press a half-hour later at his regular press conference. And, for all practical purposes, that was the end of the story.

It was one of the best lessons I ever learned about not beating around the bush, about telling it straight, about getting ahead of the news curve ... and mostly about how to use authority judiciously.

Over the years I have had the opportunity to work with many people in high levels of government who went to great lengths to rationalize, over explain, and generally try to off-load responsibility for decisions that they made or were part of. I've often wondered how much better off they would have been if they followed the basic principle of "get to the high ground ... as quickly as you can."

Governor Richard Snelling knew how to get to the high ground ... quickly.

A Man of Few Words

The following story is another contribution by William Gilbert, who was another of the remarkable people in and about Vermont government over the years. At one point he found himself serving as Governor Snelling's legal counselor in the mid 1970s.

There came a moment during that period when Bill gave a not very good interview with the *Burlington Free Press*. In Bill's view, the quote itself was accurate, but it was also very clear that what Bill said was, in his words, "… stupid and made the Governor look not quite in command of the subject at hand."

Governor Snelling had a basic rule for staff, and that was to read the *Free Press* first thing every morning, with the expectation that anything

that needed to be fixed could be dealt with by the time the day was over. In this particular case the Governor was not pleased with Bill's quote. As the Governor's General Counsel, Bill was held to a very high standard in his work and interaction with the media.

Bill describes his anxiety as he went into the daily morning staff meeting. These meetings lasted an hour or so each day, and after the first 50 minutes without any comment from the Governor about the article, Bill began to breathe a little easier. Then, as the meeting ended, the Governor asked Bill to stay behind to discuss "something." The rest of the attuned staff knew what was coming so they fled the scene with great speed. The door closed and the Governor, sitting behind his large desk filled with the work of the day, asked Bill to sit down. An uncomfortable silence followed as he pulled out the *Free Press*, carefully clipped the article, and slowly handed it to Bill across the desk.

Before Bill could say a word, the Governor said quietly, "Bill, I know you feel badly about this article in the *Burlington Free Press*. And I do not want you to feel any worse than I do … and I feel just terrible."

That was all the Governor said. That was all he needed to say. Bill quietly limped back to his desk and resolved to be more careful and articulate when talking to the press in the future.

Bill Gilbert was known for his skill with the press for many years thereafter.

A Man Who Would Not Accept 'No'

Part of the remarkable success of Richard A. Snelling's long private sector and public career was his drive and willingness to take the extra step. Under Dick Snelling, there were no normal 8:00 A.M. to 4:00 P.M. workdays. The basic rule of thumb was that you worked until the job was completed. As a result of this philospohy, he created strong management teams that, after a period of time, began to think like the Governor. This chemistry and mentorship resulted in big achievements by his administration.

Once in a while, though, this drive for knowing where his key people were and what they were doing would get the best of him. I remember very well feeling the brunt of that one day in the fall of 1978.

Our family had taken our annual vacation at our cottage on the New Jersey shore. This was a rhythm we had established over many years. This was the time of the great striped bass fall run off the Jersey coast, and one of the prime places to catch these beauties was at the inlet at the small town of Barnegat Light, the location of our cottage.

I had left the affairs of the Department of Corrections, of which I was the Commissioner, with my remarkably effective deputy, Mr. Martin Fitzgerald. Fitzgerald was well respected in and out of government for his hard work and general dedication to the job. My mistake was that I had not notified the Governor personally that I was heading off for my family's annual vacation.

One of Governor Snelling's communication techniques was to make a telephone call directly into the bureaucracy to get an answer about something that he was thinking about. He would often avoid giving the assignment to one of his hard-working aides so that he could make the phone calls himself. He used that approach to motivate his team; and that way of doing business usually resulted in getting the information he wanted instantaneously, rather than waiting several days to receive a written memo.

Sure enough, when I was away he called my office at the then depopulated State Hospital in Waterbury, which was at the time serving as a government center, to ask me something or other.

The call went directly to Martin Fitzgerald's desk and he answered the phone. The Governor asked for me. At that point Marty uttered the fateful words, "Governor, I'm sorry, but he can't be reached."

Martin got no further with his explanation, as the Governor asked quickly, "Where is he?" Martin explained that I was on vacation with my family at the cottage in New Jersey and that there was no telephone there and that he (Martin) did not know the address.

The Governor's call to Martin was at 10 A.M. At 10:30 A.M. there was a knock on the door of the cottage. It was the New Jersey State Police. I was told that the Governor of Vermont wanted me to call him immediately. I thanked the officer and immediately drove several blocks and found a pay phone and made the call back to Vermont. (This story would not nearly be as interesting in today's instantaneous worldwide cell phone communication.)

I quickly got through to the Governor. He made no mention of the fact that he couldn't reach me in Vermont. He made no mention of what he must have done to get the New Jersey State Police to find me. He only asked me a question about some incident in corrections that was on his mind. Our conversation lasted no more than 45 seconds. At this point, many years later, I cannot even recall the content of the conversation.

What I did remember is that from then on I always notified whatever Governor I was working for when and where I would be taking my vacation, along with a direct phone number.

Deane Davis—It's the Little Things

One of the things that distinguished Governor Deane Davis from others was his personal touch.

In the mid 1970s, my wife, Jeannette, and our neighbor and my co-worker Kathie Gayer were contemplating starting a horse farm and riding center, which did, in fact, subsequently occur. The farm is in its 31st year as I write this story. This was going to be somewhat risky business, because the project would require a considerable capital expenditure for some additional land, the indoor arena, and other expensive items, such as the purchasing of horses for the school, good and safe fencing, and the like. We thought it prudent to do a statewide survey of indoor facilities in order to create a functional and efficient facility design and to take the temperature of the money requirements we would need for operating expenses.

So we began our homework, which included visiting each of the nine facilities that existed in Vermont at the time (today there are at least nine facilities in Washington County alone). We also undertook a rough horse census in Washington County in order to determine the level of horse activity. We sent a mail survey to anyone we could think of, or the UVM Extension Service could think of, who was involved with horses in any way, to determine what kind of market might exist of people who might purchase our services.

We received a set of enthusiastic responses which we were able to take to the bank, as we were now borrowing a considerable sum to get the project off the ground.

One of those responses was a handwritten letter from ex-Governor Deane C. Davis, who was a renowned horseman in Washington County and beyond. His love for the all-purpose and sturdy Vermont Morgan horse was well known. Following is his note in full:

"Because I expect to be out of state winters, this program does not fit my needs. However, if it can be produced it would fill a long felt need for horse people in the area. A very few years ago I would have been personally interested. The lack of winter facilities is a great gap in this climate. More power to you. … Deane Davis."

This little note sealed the deal for us. This was typical of the personal approach of Deane Davis and was one of the reasons why he was held in such high esteem and regard by the people of Vermont.

INK

Because I expect to be out of state winters, this program does not fit my needs. However, if it can be produced, it would fill a long-felt need for horse

Strange Things Happen When It Gets Cold in Vermont

Some funny things can happen in Vermont when it gets very cold. I remember well a stretch of deep February cold in the early 1980s when the temperature never went above 0 for 12 days. On several occasions during that time it plunged to 30 degrees below zero, and it even reached 40 below at one point.

Heading out at 5:00 A.M. one morning for a plane ride out of Burlington, my wife and I were listening to the redoubtable and irrepressible Bob Bannon on his early morning radio show on WSKI. Bob was taking calls from different places in Washington County from listeners who were giving him the coldest temperature readings. There was one caller who claimed that on the south side of his house it was 35 below, while on the north side of the house it was 40 below.

Coming back from this particular trip, the cold had not let up. It was a cloudless Saturday morning and the temperature was still a bone-numbing 25 below zero.

Our family was being visited that weekend by an old college friend, Bob Dreyer, who at the time was living in New Jersey. Dreyer proudly owned a wonderful diesel Mercedes Benz. When he went to start it that morning, it simply groaned once and quit. Our plan was to tow his car with a tractor (that had spent the night covered with a blanket under which there was a lit 60 watt bulb) owned by Joe Griffith, our farmer neighbor across the road, to the large garage around the corner next to the home of old-timer Lynn Copeland. At the garage, we would light up Lynn's old wood furnace to warm up the technological marvel of this diesel sedan.

During this episode, we were again listening to the legendary Bob Bannon's morning show. Another of Bannon's routines was to dial up the local police stations to get firsthand accounts of what went on in Montpelier and Barre the evening before. We caught an interesting conversation.

The Montpelier police chief had answered the phone, and the one-way conversation was going something like this:

Bob Bannon: "Anything going on in Montpelier last night ... that's right, it was very cold ... so things were pretty quiet? ... Oh, you had a streaker in town last night? ... Wasn't it kind of cold to be streaking? ... 28 below ... that is cold. What did you do with the streaker? Put him in the back of the squad car? ... OOOOOH, the squad car had plastic seats eh ... I'll bet he was glad to get to the jail ..."

Further down the road as we were towing the Mercedes, we came to Gary Bernier's house, which was just across from our horse stables. Gary was a UPS driver and owned a large Chevy Suburban van. He evidently had trouble starting it also. As we approached his driveway, we could see some smoke and even flame licking up from under the van along the doors. We rushed to the van to see if there was anything we could do to put out the fire under the van. And there was Gary, sitting in the driver's seat.

Gary rolled the window down when he saw us. He told us not to worry, that he had built a fire underneath the van in order to soften the oil in the oil pan beneath the car, and when it was soft enough, he would start the van and drive away from the fire.

Needless to say, our two visiting friends were dumbstruck. But sure enough a couple of minutes later, when the flames were now a good third of the way up the side of the van, Gary turned the key, the van started, and he drove off of the fire and down the road to work.

Like I said ... some strange things can happen when it gets cold in Vermont.

It's Miller Time

Richard "Dick" Turner had a full career working for the Vermont Department of Corrections. At one point in that career he found himself working as the Superintendent of the Chittenden Correctional Facility. This is a facility with almost 200 inmates, some of whom live in a maximum security area. Escapes are rare in this type of facility, but occasionally they do happen.

On New Year's Eve in 1982, Dick Turner was off duty, partying with friends and family. At about 10:00 P.M., two inmates from the maximum security area successfully breached security by breaking their way out through a skylight in the security area. Within seconds after reaching the outside, they were over the razor-ribboned barbed wire fence and gone into the surrounding neighborhood.

The police and media were notified, and a call was put into Dick, who immediately proceeded to the prison to take charge and be available to reporters, who would soon be calling demanding details about the escape and information about the inmates regarding their degree of dangerousness and the potential for violence as they were hunted by the police and correction officers.

Dick arrived at the facility in, shall we say, a state that was close to inebriation as a result of the partying that he was involved with while off duty earlier in the evening.

At the same time, WCAX—predominant television station serving most of Vermont—arrived with their electronic satellite truck. The station headquarters was only minutes from the correctional facility, so they arrived quickly. The facility staff was preoccupied with state police in mapping out the process for the search, which was just getting under way. They had not yet taken the time to put together a press release with the basic facts of who, what, when, and where. Therefore, it fell to Dick to appear on camera with the WCAX reporter, who was thirsting for the inside scoop and all of the detail, for the station's viewers.

The camera was quickly set up in the Superintendent's office, and soon thereafter, Dick Turner appeared.

Those who saw Dick at that precise moment should have known that he was not in the best shape to be on camera. His eyes were a little glazed, and he his words were somewhat slurred. He was a bit unsteady on his feet; but he had no choice. The reporter was not to be denied.

The interview began with the basics. "What time did the escape occur?" asked the reporter. "10:07 P.M.," said Dick. "From what part of the facility did they escape?" "The high security section," said Dick. "How did they get out?" "Through a skylight," said Dick.

So far so good. Any viewer watching was getting the straight scoop in a direct manner.

However, the next question elicited a very different kind of response. "Why did these men leave the facility?" asked the reporter. Dick gazed at the camera for a moment, then finally uttered the following—"It's Miller Time"—to the astonishment of all of those watching. Anyone who had seen Dick's unsteadiness and glazed eyes understood immediately.

The good news for the Department of Corrections and the Governor's Office was that very few people were watching television news that evening. People were out having a good time, partying with friends and family, and the last thing folks had any interest in was watching the 11:00 P.M. news.

This story gained legendary status over the years. It was a story that Dick never lived down. It was just one of those delicious moments.

'Perfect'

In about 1984, I was deeply enmeshed as CEO of a direct mail firm in Montpelier, International Coins and Currency. The company had been plunged into Chapter Eleven in 1980, and was in the final throes of completing a reorganization plan. This plan was to be submitted to the courts, banks, and creditors, aiming for final approval by the bankruptcy court to be considered "rehabilitated" and ready to continue as a going business outside the supervision of the Vermont bankruptcy court.

At about that time I received a heads-up call from Governor Snelling's Secretary of Administration, Mr. David Wilson. David was a very highly regarded attorney practicing in Montpelier, who also had a long and distinguished career in Vermont's State government. He was calling me to warn me that I would be receiving a telephone call from Governor Snelling, who was looking for a citizen chair of the Vermont Lottery Commission.

Given the intensity of my work at the time as we were slowly moving toward discharge of the court, I was reluctant to take on any assignment that could take my eye off the important business ball in play. And, I was not a fan of the lottery. Up to that point the lottery was a low-key affair in Vermont, and there were public rumblings that the legislature might be making a move to expand Vermont's lottery by joining the newly forming "Tri-State Lottery," which would be composed of the northern tier states of Maine, New Hampshire, and possibly Vermont.

I thanked David for the heads-up, knowing that I had to prepare for the call, which the Governor would probably make over the next day or so, because this issue was on his mind.

I prepared carefully by thinking through all of the factors, and then I decided to decline the Governor's offer. I reduced my thoughts onto a single three by five card, knowing the Governor would get right to the point and that I needed to have a ready answer. Also, the idea of writing my response down was to make sure that I did not wither or wilt under

Governor Snelling's well-known persuasiveness and the power of his personality, which was legend.

Sure enough, early the next day the call came in ... and I was ready.

The Governor began, "Con, I'm calling you to ask you, at least part time, to come back into public service. I need you to serve as the citizen chair of the Vermont Lottery. I need someone I can trust who can represent my views about the lottery and, given its probable political reality, I need a chair who I believe can help keep the enterprise squeaky clean. And, you, and any citizen who is called to serve by any governor, has a duty to serve." The Governor was on a roll, and for a moment I felt myself beginning to acquiesce. But just in time I looked at the three by five card and regained my senses.

When the Governor finished his request (read "demand"), I responded. Reading word for word from the card I said, "Governor, I am flattered and pleased that you would think I could do a good job for you on this issue; however, I am not a fan of the lottery. I believe it preys on those who can least afford it, and the data from other states show that there is about a 5% addiction rate. (I also knew that the Governor loved a data-based argument and felt that it could only add to my position.) But most importantly I simply do not want to spend my time being responsible for the overall conduct and operation of a public gambling operation."

Inside I was smiling. I knew that I had been more prepared for the conversation than the Governor had been. That was until I heard the one word that changed the dynamics of the conversation completely. From the other end of the phone came the word "perfect ... you will be the perfect chair."

And so, that is how I became the Chair of the Vermont Lottery, a position I held for several years until Governor Richard Snelling decided not to run again and left office in 1985.

Here's What I Think of the Lottery Bill

I need to inform the reader about how much the Governor detested the lottery to make the above story come alive. When the tri-state bill finally passed overwhelmingly in the Vermont Legislature, it came time for the Governor to sign the bill. Under the law, the Governor could simply not sign the bill, and still the bill would become law. However, Governor Snelling had a practice of signing almost every bill passed by the legislature even though it had a veto-proof majority, in his knowledge that a bill passed by the Legislature was the law, and that as Governor, he had a responsibility to sign it into law.

The day that the Governor decided to sign the lottery bill, he was working in the Governor's ceremonial office in the State House. That room is one of the most interesting and spectacular rooms in our venerable State House. It is filled with paintings from the masters and has ornate woodwork encircling the entire room. Unnoticed in the room to most people is a movable panel, behind which is a very small bathroom, built into the wall for the convenience of Governors, who could use the room discretely, and not have to use the public bathrooms in the main hallway of the State House, when they did not have the time to get engaged in long conversations with legislators and lobbyists, which is inevitable when they roam the State House.

The story goes that on the day the lottery bill was to be signed, the Governor invited several reporters and key staffers into the tiny bathroom, and proceeded to sit down on the closed toilet, and then uttered "This is what I think about the lottery bill," as he signed the bill.

Governor Snelling truly did not like the Lottery.

Neil and the .22

Once in a while, as a father, you can luck into a situation that has long-term benefit. When our son, Neil, was 13, he found an old .22 long Ruger in my gun closet. It was a gun I had acquired when I was a correction officer in New Jersey. I hadn't used it in about 15 years. Years earlier I had used it for target practice.

Neil asked about the history of the gun, which I shared with him. He then asked if he could learn to shoot it, and the answer was, of course, yes.

We spent some time taking the gun apart and cleaning and oiling it. Then we went through some important safety rules. Finally, we set up a target below the house. Behind the house was a downward sloping field for about 50 yards, followed by a sharp wooded rise. We set up a target about 50 feet from the house. I purchased some boxes of .22 long shells, gave Neil some basic shooting instructions and let him go at it.

The first few times out, it was easy to see how quickly he was improving. On his third practice session he decided to put the target a good 40 yards down the field, except this time the target was an empty tin can stuck upside down on a stick. It wasn't long before he became somewhat frustrated, because he just couldn't hit the target. By and by, Neil came into the house to tell me that there was something wrong with the gun. I tried to tell him that the target was simply too far away, and that he had to increase the distance from the place of the first target by increments. But he wasn't having any of it. His belief was that, just because he could hit the target at 50 feet (and that was no small accomplishment), he should be able to hit it at 120 feet.

So I went outside with him and watched him shoot through another 20 rounds or so with no luck, at which point he gave me the gun to try it. Now I hadn't shot a handgun for many years, and I certainly knew that I wasn't going to hit the target. But I thought if I shot and missed that he would get the idea that he had to bring the target much closer.

So I took the gun and, most casually, without any kind of proper aim or preparation, snapped off a single shot. Amazingly, the can jumped off the stick. Neil ran down the field, grabbed the can, and ran back to the house. With some awe in his voice he showed me that not only had I hit the can, but I had hit it dead center, as the bullet hole was perfectly placed through the center of the can.

It was all I could do to keep a straight face. I simply told Neil that there was nothing wrong with the gun and that he simply had to keep practicing.

Neil was truly impressed with his father. His dad really knew how to shoot. That little event laid the groundwork for several years of a terrific relationship with my son.

Asparagus

In *Met Along the Way,* I lightly introduced you to Peter "Curly" Griffith, our neighbor, who was Joe Griffith's father and who had quite a colorful history. By the time we got to know Curly, he was well into his 80s and spent considerable time puttering in the old shop that had served as a maintenance shed when the farm was operating and in full bloom.

On our occasional visits to the Griffiths' home on cold winter evenings, we learned a lot about Curly and his wife, Annie, and the life that they led in Detroit before they moved to East Hill in Plainfield in 1927.

In the old tin-ceilinged dining room and on the wall over the old Glenwood wood-fired oven was an old copper-tipped wooden airplane propeller. The propeller was from Curly's days as a young man in the mid 1920s, when he was a personal pilot for Henry Ford. Curly's job for Mr. Ford was to fly paperwork for the Ford Motor Company all across the country. Curly loved to recount how on a flight from, say, Detroit to Maine he would find a relatively flat piece of farm real estate where he would land his plane, pay the farmer for a tankful of gas, and then pay for an overnight stay in the farmer's house, which included a dinner with the family and an early morning farm breakfast, followed by a quick lift-off to continue on his way, for example, to the coast of Maine. Curly certainly led a carefree and full life.

One early spring day in the mid 1980s, my wife, Jeannette, and I were preparing an asparagus bed when we saw Curly crossing Gonyeau Road to where we were working on the garden. "Whatcha doin'?" asked Curly. "We're planting asparagus," Jan replied. With those two words, Curly launched into a stream-of-consciousness monologue that must have lasted nonstop, seemingly without a breath, for 15 minutes. The story started in Marian, Illinois, where he picked up some paperwork to fly back to St. Louis, where he delivered the information and picked up additional paperwork then he flew back south to Carbondale, Illinois, only to drop off and pick up more paper as he continued his never-ending up and down journey. He told us how much gas he needed to get from here to there. He told us who the people were and how friendly they were at each stop, and which ones he could trust and which ones he could not. He told us what the weather was on each of the multiple flight legs. He told us about the engine foibles and anomalies and how he could spot a good mechanic from the air. The torrent of information was intense and unending.

Jan and I sat on the ground transfixed at this flow of information that was being transmitted to us with no pause in sight.

Finally, Curly simply said, "My last leg of the trip that day was back to Detroit, where I brought home a small load of asparagus ..."—at which point he wheeled on his heel and marched across Gonyeau Road back to his home.

I learned a lot of what some people might call useless information from Curly during his last years. But Jeannette and I savored every bit of his life's experience.

Governor Snelling's Late Musings

Governor Richard A. Snelling had his fatal heart attack in August of 1991.

During his first eight years in office in the late 1970s and early 1980s, he was known as a hard-charging businessman who, in the words of Sister Elizabeth Candon, his Secretary of Human Services, "did not suffer fools gladly." He was a tightly organized man who ran government like he ran his business, Shelburne Industries, over the years.

Working for Dick Snelling was not easy. He wasn't a micro-manager per se, but part of his management style was to know everything that occurred in an agency and, more importantly, why it occurred. Many good young people who served him in various capacities suffered under that regimen (although, virtually all would readily volunteer that they learned much under the Governor's tutelage).

So it was with a sense of quiet surprise for those of us who came to work for him during his revival period as Governor in 1991 that Richard Snelling was quite a different man, with a softer style than in his first round of service.

This sense of relative mellowness did not dampen his fire for excellence and logic in the work of government, but it did mean that his relationships with the people who worked with him in his second round of service were much more enjoyable for those around him. In my mind, this subtle shift was evident in a new wrinkle in his after-work Thursday informal meetings with his key staff. Basically, sometime during a Wednesday, the Governor would ask his long-standing secretary, Jeannie Johnson, to make a few calls into the agencies to invite some of his key people to his office on the fifth floor of the Pavilion after working hours on Thursday evening. Some of the people who would periodically attend included Dick Chapman, the Governor's Secretary of Administration; Doug Wacek, the Budget Director; Jan Eastman, his Environmental Secretary; Tom Moore, the Secretary of Civil and Military Affairs; Elizabeth

"Wibs" Edwards, the Chief of Staff; Jack Tenney, the Governor's fiscal advisor; Pat Garahan, the Transportation Secretary; me, and others. We all would not be at every meeting, but some cross-section of the above group would always be present.

At the meeting there was always a bottle of Wild Turkey, provided by the Governor, sitting on the coffee table.

There was no formal agenda. We talked about whatever the people attending and the Governor would want to talk about, in or out of government. They were fascinating conversations because we got to understand better what made each of the Governor's key people tick, and it certainly helped in forming a strong sense of team. (This sense of team would unexpectedly come to the forefront at the time of the Governor's death when the new and unexpected Governor, Howard Dean, would keep almost the entire cabinet team together as he began his cycle of governance during a difficult period of recession and potential uncertainty after Governor Snelling's death.)

They were great discussions, but the ones I remember most vividly were the musings of Governor Snelling himself. One of his recurring themes was his worry that our democracy and methods of decision-making were not increasing adequately to deal with the increasing complexity and demands of issues that were facing our country and state. He would chronicle the ways in which our country could wait, historically, until there was a crisis and then how we would launch into a problem-solving mode to fix the problem. Americans are inveterate problem-solvers, he would recount.

His concern was that there were issues brewing on the horizon that were so large and complex that they rendered the current problem-solving mode not workable. One of those issues was the growing (and invisible to most Americans) national debt—an issue on which the Governor had spent so much time after his defeat in his run for the U.S. Senate against Senator Patrick Leahy. Health care, which was turning into another growing and ever more complex issue, was another concern of his. He was becoming less sure that our current process of governance and decision-making could solve these problems.

This was a different picture and side of Richard Snelling than any of us who had worked for him before had seen. It was an introspective, worried, and sincerely probing set of concerns. He would quietly challenge each of us on these and other subjects during these gatherings.

I've often wondered what he would be thinking about regarding these same issues, in view the political paralysis associated with them in today's politics.

A Remarkable Memory

The day that Governor Richard Snelling died marked a significant moment in Vermont. That morning I was at the Top Notch resort in Stowe with Richard Mills, the long-standing Commissioner of Education, giving a joint talk to a group of early childhood practitioners when a note was handed to me that simply said, "Governor Snelling has died." There are not words enough to describe the shock and hurt. Later that day, Howard Dean, Vermont's Lieutenant Governor, was sworn in as the Governor of the State.

Early the next day, I received a call from Wibs Edwards, Governor Snelling's Chief of Staff, that the new Governor wanted to meet with each of the cabinet members later in the day.

I was in no shape to make a presentation about the activities and priorities of the Agency of Human Services, so I decided to simply make a list of 50 key words that I would use to trigger my thoughts to the Governor and hope that they would be coherent and clear enough to be useful to him. The list included words such as welfare reform, corrections, Brandon (the state's school for the developmentally disabled), child support, Medicaid, mental health, and so on. I had asked the Chief Administrator for the Agency, Peter Profera, to accompany me to the meeting with Governor Dean (up to that moment I had never met Dean). My instruction to Peter was to simply watch and listen, and then after we left the meeting to let me know how much of the complex material that I had tried to convey was understood.

We met that day with the Governor in the State House. He was alone with no staff or other assistance. I used the key words to trigger as much information as I could muster. Governor Dean said very little. He simply listened intently. At the end of the meeting, he thanked Peter and me, and we left the building.

On the way down the long steps in front of the State House I asked Peter how much of the 45-minute rambling presentation I had made got through to Howard Dean. Did the Governor understand fully what I was telling him, or was it going past him? Peter simply said to me that Howard Dean had understood and comprehended every word.

Future interaction with the Governor would bear out Peter's impression. Things that I had told the Governor in that emotionally charged meeting would be recalled and referred to by the Governor regularly. Facts and figures would be recounted by him in our policy discussions. As time went on, Governor Dean would exhibit over and over his grasp of complex detail. I attributed this remarkable capacity to his training as a physician. Physicians are expected to recall huge amounts of information and data at a moment's notice. Physicians are, in effect, walking encyclopedias of detailed information.

This capacity served Howard Dean well in the information-rich environment of government and politics.

Lady Jeannette

So far I've avoided putting my wife, Jeannette, into any of these stories. But I think it is time.

Jan and I knew each other in high school, in Burlington, New Jersey, in the late 1950s. During our college years we spent considerable time together on the Jersey shore and found ourselves getting tangled romantically. We were married in 1965, and we began our lives together. As I moved into public service over the years, Jeannette found herself a partner in East Hill Farm Family Riding Center, which we established in 1976 with Kathie Gayer, an accomplished horsewoman who had hooked our daughter on horses at a very young age. Kathie later married Bill Moulton, a forester, and the four of us have had a long-term successful business relationship revolving around the farm.

Having two families involved with the farm, and now three families— as our daughter, Ruth, and her husband, Bo Poulsen, a talented Dane who is a farrier by trade, have joined the business—has allowed each family the freedom to do some occasional traveling, which each of us has taken advantage of over the years.

In 1999, through a set of interesting circumstances, I found myself, after nine years as Vermont's Secretary of Human Services, invited to a remarkable meeting in England. The remarkableness of the meeting had less to do with the content than where it was to be held, namely inside Windsor Castle, one of the homes of the Queen. It was to be a meeting of a very few people who worked in the field of human services from six different countries. Each country was to send one delegate to the meeting, plus a representative of a foundation from each country. And our wives were also invited to attend.

We soon found ourselves inside the walls of the castle and staying in the spare accommodations of the Saint George House. The Saint George House was located just next to the Saint George Chapel, home to the Knights of the Garter, where every morning the boys' choir would sing

as part of the daily morning prayer. It was really a magical three days. The meeting itself was held in the castle library, which had volumes of books and texts that were written as far back as the mid 1400s.

The library, the living quarters of the Queen (who was not in residence at the time), the Saint George House, and other parts of the castle were clearly marked as off limits to the general public, but not off limits to those of us at the conference.

Jan took full advantage of her time while the small meeting of twelve unfolded over the three days. As a temporary resident of the castle, she had much more freedom to roam the grounds and the surrounding estates and farms associated with the castle.

One day after her wanderings, she walked back into the castle through the main gate, past the Queen's guard and across the courtyard, which was semi-crowded with tourists, to a large old black chain that served to demarcate the public from the private part of the castle. As she opened the chain to walk through, she heard an American woman ask her companion, "I wonder who that person is who is going behind the chain." Without missing a beat, Jeannette wheeled around and curtsied, while at the same time she said, "Why, I'm Lady Jeannette of Plainfield." This showy bit is so unlike my wife. It was as if she had been possessed by a sense of her special status and privilege of the moment. She was absolutely aglow when I met her a few minutes later. She was experiencing a mixture of embarrassment and chagrin, and yet at the same time exhilaration as a result of the moment and the place.

The wonderful experience we had is always more intensely relived when we think about Lady Jeannette.

Joe, It Was So Good To See You

This next story is written with sincere affection for the longtime public-serving Jim Jeffords.

I had been a Jim Jeffords watcher since 1971 when he was Vermont's Attorney General and I was the Deputy Commissioner of Corrections. At that time it was clear to everyone that Jim was on the political move. You could see it in his considerable and public disagreements with Governor Davis, which I remember vividly during contentious monthly meetings of what was then known as the Emergency Board, the out-of-session legislative and executive group to which the Legislature granted certain decision-making powers. This was also the period of an active federal funder, the Law Enforcement Assistance Administration, a provision under which Attorney General Jeffords had a seemingly never-ending set of funding requests for his office and law enforcement agencies across the State. It was a very visible and productive time for the Attorney General. During that time I came to know Mr. Jeffords tangentially in my role as Deputy Commissioner of Corrections.

My next round of interaction with Jim Jeffords (by this time he was Senator Jim Jeffords) was in my capacity as Secretary of Human Services throughout most of the 1990s. Also, in the mid 1990s I was elected President of the American Public Welfare Association, a Washington, D.C.–based organization, comprised of the leaders of social and human services across the country. At the same time, Jim Jeffords had ascended to the Chair of the Labor Subcommittee, becoming a powerful political force, which he used well on behalf of Vermont and Vermonters.

During the 1990s I was in Washington, D.C., regularly in my APWA capacity, and virtually every visit included a visit to Senator Jeffords in the Russell Office Building. The visits with the Senator would also include Veronica Celani, who was the terrific Commissioner of Welfare when I came into office, and then later the well-known Jane Kitchel, the long-term and respected public servant from Danville, and now a State Senator from the Northeast Kingdom. Kitchel succeeded Celani, when Celani moved on to co-chair the newly formed Health Care Administration. The visits were usually tightly scripted on our part to make the best possible use of the Senator's time. He was always pleased to see Vermonters, even though our role was to constantly get as much as we could from Congress for Vermont's programs.

This was also the early period of the great national welfare debate, so our visits had not only implications for Vermont welfare policy but also national policy, given the Senator's key role on the national front.

During this period, I thought I had gotten to know Senator Jeffords pretty well, and there was little question in my mind that the Senator knew who I was and what I did in Vermont.

In 1997, Jane and I made one of our occasional trips to Washington and had scheduled some time with the Senator. It turned out to be a special meeting. Not only did the Senator want to talk about the progress of welfare reform in Vermont, which had been adopted in 1994, but he wanted to talk about a wide range of things. He had a deep interest in special education, which was well known, but not as well known was his interest in inmate education. We had a long and incisive conversation about that subject. The 20 minutes stretched to 45 minutes, and then to almost an hour. It was one of the best policy discussions one could ever wish to have with a national policy figure.

As our discussion began to wind down, he asked the photographer to come into the room, and a photo of the Senator, Jane, and me was taken. In short, the Senator had made both of us feel like most important people.

About a month later, a large brown envelope arrived in the mail at my home with the return address being the U.S. Senate. I eagerly opened the envelope to find a beautiful black and white photo of the three of us ... with the inscription, handwritten by the Senator, "It was so good to see you, Joe."

I didn't know what to think. After all these years I was sure that the Senator knew who I was. The only explanation that I could gin up for myself was that he might have confused me with an earlier corrections commissioner from that era, Joe Patrissi, and that since we were talking about corrections policy, Joe's name may have come to mind.

This was one occasion where my primary instinct was to accept the idea that it was the thought that counts.

The Jackaphesalope

Alan Miller was the perfect picture of a strapping healthy Vermont farm boy, but he was much more than that. He was also the longtime Director of Prison Industries for the Department of Corrections. He had a reputation for being creative, and he directed the many businesses that hired inmates to work during their prison stays. The list of work opportunities for inmates in the 1970s was impressive. Inmates worked in the print shop, which did much of the print work for State government; the sheet metal shop, which was the place where Vermont license plates were made; the dairy herd at the old Windsor Prison Farm; a sawmill and wood treatment plant, where railroad ties were produced and treated; an automotive repair shop that did work on State vehicles; and an upholstery repair shop, along with other trades. In those days, the work opportunities for offenders to gain skills and learn good work habits were at the center of the lives of offenders and staff in the institutions.

Alan worked in this capacity with the department until sometime in the 1980s when a major reorganization in the department de-emphasized inmate work programs. This brought an end to Alan's career in corrections in Vermont. At that point, Alan "retired" from Vermont prison work and made his way to Oklahoma, where once again he found himself running the prison work programs for the State of Oklahoma.

It was in that status that I saw Alan again in 1994, when he dropped by my office in City Center in Montpelier. I was temporarily leading the Health Care Administration and was trying to pick up the pieces after the collapse of the health care reform effort in Vermont at that time.

In his arms he brought a box that was about three-feet square. Out of the box he pulled a rather extraordinary creature, which he called a jackaphesalope. It was a stuffed, large jackrabbit with the horns of an antelope, and the wings of a pheasant. It was truly a disgusting sight, but Alan, with his strange sense of humor, had decided that this should be something that adorned my desk. And saying "no" to Alan was a hard thing to do, simply because he was one of the nicest people you have ever met.

After the visit, Alan left to continue his trip, and the "thing" was left on my desk for me to get rid of in a way that, if the word got back to Alan, he wouldn't be too disappointed.

The secretarial staff took an instant dislike to this abomination. I had one female employee file a grievance because the stuffed animal made her physically ill to look at. And, from that day forth, she wouldn't do anything that required her to be inside my office. Another employee filed a grievance purporting that the stuffed animal triggered serious allergies.

I was truly in a fix.

About then, my time with the Health Care Administration was coming to a close. Governor Dean had found Theresa Alberghini, of Senator Leahy's Washington, D.C., staff, to serve as the next full-time director of the organization. That freed me to go back full time to the Agency of Human Services as Secretary. So one afternoon, I moved the few possessions that I had in my City Center office, including the jackaphesalope, in the battered box that it had arrived in, back to my permanent office at the agency in Waterbury.

At the end of my first day back, I stayed late, because I had a plan for the "thing." The Department of Fish and Game was in the same sprawling building that the Agency of Human Services and its departments called home. After the work day was over, I strolled my way to the office of the Fish and Game Commissioner, the likable Mr. Al Elzer, who, given his Montana raising and roots, figured to have a sense of humor about something as grotesque as the JPL (short for jackaphesalope).

The Fish and Game Department had a well-stocked trophy case just outside Commissioner Elzer's office. In the case were taxidermy figures. There was a white fox, a stuffed snowy owl, various large rodents, a fisher cat, a coyote, and a variety of other well-preserved critters indigenous to Vermont. I gently moved enough of the animals around to make enough room for the JPL. It was really a complement to the other stuffed animals, and it blended right into its new home.

Several weeks went by before I began to hear anything about it. The Waterbury government center has a large cafeteria where many employees gather for lunch. Quite a few of the commissioners from the various departments would eat there and take advantage of the time with other commissioners to get some of their joint thinking done. Al Elzer was openly trying to find out who left the JPL in his department's trophy case. He was now getting employee complaints about the JPL, but different kinds of complaints than I had received in Montpelier. His organization was complaining about the lack of respect that someone must have for the wonderful natural animals of Vermont that had been stuffed and put into the case.

Finally, someone put two and two together, and one evening, toward the end of the day, came Al Elzer with the JPL in the ratty box that I had brought it over in. The jig was up.

Now I was back to my original dilemma ... what to do with the thing.

At that point I had a marvelous thought. I roughly sealed the ratty box and addressed it to Mr. Bob Rogan, who at that time was Governor Dean's Chief of Staff. I inserted a note into the box with the following message: "Bob, this is what the Governor's health plan is beginning to look like,"—hoping that both Bob and the Governor would have the appropriate sense of humor. The next day the box was on its way.

What I did not know was that two days before I sent the box to Mr. Rogan, the State Police had just conducted a training program for all of the personnel on the fifth floor of the Pavilion, which included the Governor's staff, about how to recognize a suspicious package that could have a bomb in it. It turns out the package met every the criteria that the staff had been drilled on. The package was sloppily put together, was wrapped rather inadequately with a sloppy tape job, was poorly addressed with scrawled penmanship, had no return address, and, simply put, looked damned suspicious.

The State Police were called, and the package was carefully taken out to the parking lot behind the Thrush Tavern, where it was very thoroughly inspected. It passed the inspection, but not without considerable consternation.

I only saw the jackaphesalope once more in Bob Rogan's office sometime later. I'll have to ask Bob one of these days (he is now Chief of Staff for newly elected Congressman Peter Welch) if by any chance it had traveled with the Dean campaign, and if there was any idea that the campaign had some resemblance to the jackaphesalope.

On second thought ... I don't think I will.

Ultimate Justice

Once in a while you have to tell a story on yourself. And I've told this story to very few people ... simply because, at the time, it had the potential to be a terrific personal embarrassment.

The story started in June of 1994 when an offshore crew of Charlie Kittridge, of Middlesex; Rob Moulton, of Rockland, Maine; Zavin Diermenjian, of Montreal; Peter Brittin, of Stowe; and I began a sailing trip on my 30-foot Ericson sloop. We left from Alburgh , Vermont, sailed down the Hudson and then along the coast to Cape May, New Jersey, then 604 miles offshore to Bermuda, then another 600 miles back to Newport, Rhode Island, and then home. It was a wonderful adventure.

There were many modifications made to the boat to make the trip safe and comfortable including the installation of a "Y" valve, which allows septic waste to be pumped directly overboard once at sea. The trip was completed in early July, and as you can imagine the boat required considerable cleaning and repairs. The sloop spent the rest of the summer and fall out of the water being restored to her Lake Champlain standard.

In early May of 1995, we put her back in the water at Mallet's Bay, and with two friends, Thurmond and Bethany Knight, took an overnight trip to the Deep Bay part of Cumberland Head in New York, north of Plattsburgh. It was very early in the season, and there were few boats in the water at that point.

After a nice sail over to the bay, we anchored up and began to settle in for the night. Soon thereafter a Clinton County Sheriff's boat came on the scene. Clinton County has a service for boaters where early in the season they will come aboard, undertake a safety and environmental inspection of the boat, and, after the boat passes muster, affix a sticker on the mast to let other law enforcement services, such as the State Police or Coast Guard, know that the boat has been inspected and approved for use in the lake.

While on board, a sheriff's deputy, as part of the standard procedure, checked the head hookup to make sure there was no overboard dumping of septic into the lake. At that point the thought struck me that I had not completely disconnected the "Y" valve after the Bermuda trip. When we came back up the Hudson River, we had turned off the valve but had not completely disconnected it, knowing that we would take care of that and other chores after the boat was hauled out of the water … but we had forgotten to do it.

Sure enough, the deputy came up from the head in the hold and told the deputy sheriff in charge that even though the "Y" valve was on the off position, it had not been disconnected. Immediately, the deputy in charge told me that I was under arrest and would now be arraigned in Clinton County Court. I was to bring my boat into the harbor behind the police boat. As you can imagine we were all quite shocked.

On the way into the harbor we took stock. Among the four of us we had $40. We also gathered the official papers from the Bermuda trip, hoping to convince someone that this was an innocent mistake.

At the dock the two deputies handcuffed me and put me in the back of a screened, locked squad car and told my wife, Jeannette, that they were taking me to the Clinton County Court House for arraignment. Once in the car I asked the deputies what was likely to happen. They matter-of-fact told me that unless I had $150 in cash that I would be jailed overnight until cash bail arrived. I was getting very nervous about this very quickly.

Then, as we were driving to the courthouse, and after a brief telephone conversation, one of the deputies told me that we were not going to the courthouse, but to the home of the magistrate on duty. We drove out to a modest home outside of town. The deputies led me to the house, where we were met by the magistrate at the front door. They led me into a small room just inside the entrance, uncuffed me, and sat me down in a wooden chair in front of an old desk with two very small flags on it, one an American flag and the other being the state flag of New York. By this time it was 9:00 P.M.

The judge asked me how I wished to plead. I answered, "Very stupid, sir." He was not amused. At that point I presented my Bermuda papers and my story. After a few moments he declared me guilty (which I was, because the rules regarding Lake Champlain are clear. If a "Y" valve is part of the septic system, it must be completely disconnected … and mine wasn't). He then told me the fine would be $120 cash, and that if I didn't have the cash I would be remanded to the Clinton County jail. I told him that I didn't have enough cash, but that I had a check. And for the first and only time in my life I made an attempt to use the possible influence of my position as Secretary of Human Services in Vermont. The judge asked why he should believe my check would be good. I went to my wallet and pulled out my State of Vermont identification card, which had been signed by Governor Howard Dean, and I told the judge that with

a phone call we could establish that my check would be a good one, as I worked directly for the Governor of the State of Vermont.

The reader can only imagine my anxiety at the time.

To my surprise, the judge thought it over and then said that he would take my check. But, he then instructed me to make it out to him personally, which I did. After paying the fine, I was taken back to the boat. The deputies watched over my shoulder as I completely disconnected the "Y" valve.

For some months I worried that somehow this episode would be found out and that I would end up in an article in the *Burlington Free Press*. I had even fantasized the headline: "Vermont Cabinet Officer Convicted of Environmental Crime." Months passed and nothing appeared, until one evening when I was watching the Channel 3 News on WCAX. Suddenly, a picture of the same judge appeared on the screen with Marcelis Parsons reporting that the judge had just been arrested for serious child abuse. It turns out that there was a young woman from Scandinavia who was living in the judge's household as an exchange student, and the judge was evidently sexually abusing the underage woman.

It was an amazing moment. I flashed back to the evening at his home, and the personal check that was required. I instantly wondered if I was but one of many persons who had gotten caught up in a scam. What I had wondered about before, I was certain of now. The judge's character had now been publicly established.

Beyond the sense of great relief that came with the revelation, I had learned a hard lesson, and I had almost paid dearly for it.

I haven't been back to Deep Bay since.

Finding the Common Ground

Finding common ground across organizations in government is often very difficult. Part of the problem is that different departments often have conflicting and incompatible legal responsibilities. There are many long-running rubs between governmental organizations, most of which never come to the attention of the general public; some others, however, are pretty well known.

For example, occasionally disputes between the Department of Corrections and the Judiciary become news, usually having to do with how a sentence imposed by the court is implemented (or not implemented) by the department. Governors that I have known have spent considerable time trying to balance the interests of the Economic and Development Agency, for example, with the Agency of Environmental Protection when the desire for economic development clashes with water-quality rules. And there are many more examples.

Late in my term as Secretary of Human Services, I was approached by Commissioner Al Elzer, the well-liked and excellent Commissioner of Fish and Wildlife.

The background for this story is that the Fish and Wildlife Department in Vermont, and in most states, raises revenue to do its good work primarily through the sale of licenses to those who fish and hunt. They receive very little money from the State's general fund. Over the years, the number of hunters, in particular, has declined significantly as our lifestyles have changed. This is a trend that the Department of Fish and Wildlife had been fighting for some years. The result of this trend was a budget that was shrinking in the face of little support from the Legislature and administrations to cover the ever-increasing revenue shortfall. This was the context for the visit that I received from Commissioner Elzer that early spring day in 1998.

Commissioner Elzer was clearly upset. It was just two weeks to the opening of fishing season, and license sales were not going well. In addition, he had just received a copy of a draft press release from the Department of Health, which, in summary, was a blunt warning to people about the potential hazards of eating fish from Vermont waters. Al knew that once this press release was published that it would hurt fishing license sales even more. He wondered if there wasn't something I could do about it in my capacity as Secretary of Human Services, which included supervision of the Department of Health.

Jan Carney was the longtime Commissioner of the Department of Health. She was a highly regarded public health physician, and she had been Commissioner for some years before I had become Secretary in 1991. Early on, Jan and I struck a bargain. The essence of the bargain was that she would provide the best science possible, and I would deal with the politics of the occasional fallout from an unpopular public health decision.

Our arrangement had worked well for a number of years. But this problem had the potential of testing that resolve.

I arranged for a meeting in my office with Jan and Al. On the appointed day, Al laid out his department's financial problems. It was clear that the impending press release would only make things worse. Jan was equally clear that her job was to warn the general public about health hazards, and that mercury levels in fish was one of those hazards.

We batted the problem around for awhile with little common ground reached. At this point, one of us (I can't recall who it was) asked the following important question: "Are there any fish that don't collect mercury, and are there any places where fish live in Vermont where mercury doesn't seem to be a problem?" I recall Jan saying that mercury doesn't seem to accumulate in Vermont streams—but it is a serious problem in Lake Champlain, the Harriman Reservoir, and other particular lakes and ponds. Al immediately saw an opening. He asked Jan if the press release could be more specific about that. Jan quickly agreed and then volunteered to offer, as part of the press release an encouragement to fathers to take their children fishing in Vermont streams, particularly for fish that don't seem to accumulate mercury, namely crappies and other pan fish.

Both of them were now getting excited because they had found some fruitful common ground. The discussion went on. A joint public relations campaign with photos of happy kids fishing in Vermont streams, along with information about how to get a child's fishing license and a notice on the poster for pregnant women and children that clearly advises them not to eat fish out of Lake Champlain or the Harriman Reservoir, was the spirit of the solution.

It was a great conclusion to a meeting that was full of potential for failure—which could have resulted in a round of ill will between two important departments of State government.

Common ground, when it can be found, can take us to new, interesting, and fruitful places, but it takes people of good will and open minds, like Al and Jan, to find it.

Bob Murray ... Over Time

Many of these short stories are written from a base of humor, and most have some kind of punch line at the end of the story. This story is not like the rest, and, in fact, was somewhat difficult to write.

When one works in corrections for too long, it is not unusual to develop a somewhat cynical and negative sense about human nature. This is because, by and large, we deal with people who have led troubled lives and who have done serious things to other people. And a few have committed crimes that are almost unspeakable, particularly when it comes to those who have taken another life.

Murderers spend most of their adult lives behind bars. Statistics tell us that nine of ten people who have murdered, have killed someone that they knew, possibly a family member or someone close to their family.

This was essentially the story of one Robert Murray, who as a young man of 20, in circumstances that we will never fully know, in the late 1950s killed a young man of 17 with a knife and then stuffed his body down a well in the Northeast Kingdom. Murray was "captured and tried" and sentenced to "a lifetime in prison" (in the words of one of the musical lines of the old folk song "The Hills of Roane County," which was based on a true story from Tennessee). In Vermont, this meant that he was sentenced to the House of Correction in old Windsor Prison for most of the rest of his life.

Murray was a man slight of build. That made him especially vulnerable to the other prisoners, who were always in the process of placing any given prisoner into his proper place in the prison's human pecking order. Murray's defense in this situation was to become known as someone who was very behaviorally unpredictable and who would not hesitate to use a knife if necessary. That perceived unpredictability, combined with a wayward eye—which put one in mind of the late character actor Jack Elam—and his gruff demeanor and personality, which exuded, "leave me alone and I'll leave you alone," served to protect Bob Murray over the years from the violence which is inevitable among inmates at the "Old Bastille" (a term that Governor Tom Salmon used at the closing of the old prison in 1974).

What does one do for 40 years in a prison where for self-protection you have isolated yourself from other people?

In Bob Murray's case he developed a skill: he became a first-class woodworker. Over the years he honed his skills to the point where, in the 1970s, Murray advertised his wares regularly in *Yankee Magazine* and had developed quite a little business. The administration at Windsor Prison recognized that this avocation not only kept Murray out of trouble at Windsor but also gave him a focus and purpose that made him easier to deal with as an inmate. The administration allowed him to bring in enough income to pay for commissary items, like cigarettes, that the prison did not pay for. It even reached the point where the administration allowed Bob to work on his projects in his cell at night and, therefore, allowed him to have quite an array of carving knives and tools in his cell. Over the years, Murray became known as being trustworthy with his tools. There was never a problem.

I had met Bob Murray in the early 1970s after he had served more than 20 years, when the parole board began the long process of consideration for a supervised parole sometime in the undefined future. Through that process I got to know him quite well. When I left the Corrections Department in the late 1970s, we continued to correspond. It was through that correspondence that I began to see the softer side of Bob. And since I was no longer part of the system, there was no reason for Bob to be manipulating me, which is always a potential danger. During the 1980s when I was out of government, Bob had made several tries for parole and had actually been placed under tight furlough supervision in the Chittenden County area on two occasions, only to fail each time. He had been in prison so long that he found it hard to make even the most minor adjustments to life on the outside.

Over the course of the 1990s, when I came back into government in human services and Windsor Prison had been long closed, Bob was an inmate at the St. Albans Correctional Facility, where, once again, he was having difficulty. The inmates there were much younger than Bob, and he didn't have the privileges at St. Albans that he had at the old prison.

But Bob was now in his 60s, and his health was beginning to fail. And as Secretary of the Agency that had ultimate responsibility for the Department of Corrections, there was little I could do for him, lest I be tagged with using the influence of my office on his behalf, which is simply the wrong thing to do.

After I left government again in 1999, the department was trying to release him once again. This time, it was decided that he would be released to the Northeast Kingdom in the Lyndonville area. This was a part of the State that Bob felt comfortable in, and he was adjusting much better. I staked him for some woodworking equipment, and he found a trailer to live in. For several years he would work on his projects during the winter and then set up a table alongside the road in the warmer months, selling his carvings and tables to tourists. He was doing very well, and for the first time he was leading what most of us would consider to be a normal life.

By now Bob was almost 70, and it was clear that his health was in serious decline. In the winter of 2003, Bob caught pneumonia and, after a short time, he died.

In this account I'm realizing that I've covered most of a life span in the space of a couple of pages. I haven't come close to capturing the dynamics of Bob's life, but I do know that over the course of the years Bob fundamentally changed from an angry, alcohol-ridden, dangerous young man to a thoughtful, talented, kind person. If only we had the key to accelerating that kind of human change.

I have often thought about the untapped talent that is inherent in the thousands of prisoners who move through our correctional system—and the utter waste of it all.

And ... I wonder what Bob would think if he read this.

Afterword

Also Met Along the Way was a result of the many letters I received after publishing the original *Met Along the Way*. I received letters from Mr. William Cowles, who was featured in the first book and who supplied me with other memorable moments from his time in government. The well-known Bill Gilbert, who also served for many years in many different capacities in government also weighed in with stories and memories. I even received a letter from a woman from Montpelier who regaled me with her memories of having an apartment in the 1940s that overlooked the wall at Windsor Prison. The letter was filled with her memories of the inmates regularly batting their softballs over the wall and through her glass windows as part of the games within the walls, and how there was a team of inmates that would immediately come up to her apartment to fix the window, and receiving milk and cookies for their effort.

We all have our favorite stories about life. My hope is that these little books will serve to trigger others to take the time to write them down and share them. It is these moments that result in a deeper understanding of the humanity that in one way or another binds us all.

Con Hogan